Say It Like Shakespeare

*How to Give a Speech Like Hamlet,
Persuade Like Henry V, and Other Secrets
From the World's Greatest Communicator*

Thomas Leech

McGraw-Hill

New York   Chicago   San Francisco
Lisbon   London   Madrid   Mexico City   Milan   New Delhi
San Juan   Seoul   Singapore   Sydney   Toronto

To Leslie and Marla,
my wife and daughter,
who constantly add spark to both
my professional and personal lives.

McGraw-Hill

*A Division of The **McGraw·Hill** Companies*

1 2 3 4 5 6 7 8 9 0   DOC/DOC   0 9 8 7 6 5 4 3 2 1

ISBN 0-07-137315-2

Printed and bound by R.R. Donnelley & Sons Company. McGraw-Hill books are available at special quantity discounts to use as premiums and sales promotions, or for use in corporate training programs. For more information, please write to the Director of Special Sales, Professional Publishing, McGraw-Hill, Two Penn Plaza, New York, NY 10121-2298. Or contact your local bookstore.

This book is printed on recycled, acid-free paper containing a minimum of 50% recycled, de-inked fiber.

Contents

Acknowledgments   v

Part I: The Path to Better Communication   1

1. Why the Bard as Communication Guru?   3

2. Exceeding Wise or Counterfeit Rascal: What's Your Personal Scorecard?   13

3. Mend Your Speech a Little: Ready to Go?   23

Part II: The Sender's Role   35

4. Speak the Speech, Trippingly: Tune Up That Voice   37

5. Speak Plain and to the Purpose: Enhancing Language Power   47

6. Is Your English Frittered? Overcoming Language Deficiencies   61

7. Suit the Action to the Word: Body Language That Works for You   79

8. Let the Apparel Proclaim the Man (and Woman): Appearance as a Positive Factor   97

9. Get into a Winning State of Mind   107

Part III: The Receiver and Feedback Roles   117

10. Bestow the Sense of . . . Hey There, Are You Listening?   119

CONTENTS

11. Receiver Meets Sender in Q&A   135

12. Test the Verbosity to the Argument: Sharpen Your Critical Listening Skill   145

Part IV: Getting a Good Message   151

13. Tuning In: First, Do Your Homework   153

14. To Speak and Purpose Not? Set Your Approach   165

15. Bait the Hook Well: Organize Your Material   175

16. Let Us Tell Sad Stories: Develop the Substance   189

Part V: The Medium Supports the Message   207

17. Alas, Poor Yorick: Apply Visual Aids Well   209

18. Silence That Dreadful Bell! Use the Medium Wisely   223

Part VI: Competitive Communication   239

19. Gather Your Team: Once More unto the Breech!   241

20. The Readiness Is All: Prepare Well   253

21. Unveil That Knave! This Is a Competition   263

22. A Hit, a Very Palpable Hit! You Won!   271

23. Done to Death by Slanderous Tongues! Uh-oh, You Lost   277

Part VII: Continuing Onward   287

24. Speak—It's Your Cue: Moving Forward   289

Credits   293

Index of Famous Lines   299

Index   301

Acknowledgments

I have relied on many sources in researching this fascinating subject: books, videos, audios, and performances of many plays I have seen at the San Diego Old Globe Theater, The Delacorte Theater in New York City's Central Park, and theaters at Stratford, Connecticut; Purdue University; and elsewhere. Because the language—words and punctuation—varies from source to source, I have relied on one primary style guideline: the tattered, yellowed book I've been dipping in and out of many years, the 1936 edition of *The Complete Works of William Shakespeare* (edited by William Addis Wright, Garden City Books, NY).

Through the many live performances of Shakespeare I've seen, some stand out for incredible power, the sort that keep coming to mind a decade or two later. These performers provided memorable evenings and vividness about the power of the characters and words of Shakespeare: Anthony Zerbe as Iago, Victor Buono (at age 19) as Falstaff; James Earl Jones as Othello; Jacqueline Brooks as Cleopatra; Morris Carnovsky as Shylock; and Jonathan McMurtry as many characters.

Also highly valuable to me has been my sounding board of reviewers and critics: Leslie Johnson-Leech, Seymour Zeenkov, Jack Farnan, and Pamela Adams, all Hamlet's "Wisest friend [who] shall hear and judge." Their counsel has been sound and much of it even incorporated into this book, although they are in no way to blame for any perceived remaining deficiencies. Thanks, too, to Mary Glenn and Scott Amerman and the rest of the editing and production team at McGraw-Hill for their guidance and skill in getting this from manuscript to bound book.

To all of the above, borrowing from *Twelfth Night*'s Sebastian: "I can no other answer make but thanks and thanks and ever. . . ."

Part I

❦

The Path to Better Communication

The Merchant of Venice. 2, 2

In Part I you are asked to take a fresh look at how communication fits into your business and personal worlds. Then you are shown how to size up how you might rank on a communication scorecard. And finally you are urged to commit to your own communication improvement program (and then to enjoy the rewards that follow).

Chapter 1

Why the Bard as Communication Guru?

> No man is the lord of any thing,
> Though in and of him there be much consisting,
> Till he communicate his parts to others.
>
> Ulysses, *Troilus and Cressida*. 3, 3

We strive mightily to enhance our communication ability. As we do so, we look to various gurus and sources of wisdom for inspiration. How about you? Have you sat through company training seminars? Attended college extension classes? Picked up books on office communication or business presentations (and actually read them)? Been coached, like it or not, by upper managers or outside consultants? Joined your local Toastmasters Club? Even started dressing for success? All these efforts for self-improvement try to absorb and apply the latest hot stuff. If you do any of these, good for you.

You can also gain much insight into communicating effectively by heeding the advice of a chap named William Shakespeare, who achieved lasting fame several centuries back as a writer, not a communication guru. Even so, the Bard of Avon wove many observations pertinent to communicating into his tales of high intrigue and low comedy.

 3

Bid me discourse, I will enchant thine ear.

Venus and Adonis. 145

As you read Shakespeare's observations, you'll see how they readily apply to many forms of communication involved in the workplace—for example, meetings, written reports, presentations, customer service, managing, giving feedback, e-mail, and task teams. They also apply to the many skills that make communication work or fail—for example, language, voice, nonverbal communication, appearance, listening, and relationships.

Do these skills sound like they have application outside the workplace, such as at home, social gatherings, or meetings of your condo association, local service club, or political group? You bet.

You may or may not be a devotee of the Bard, yet his words will trigger some "Aha's!," give you a refreshing (and catchy) perspective about many facets of communication, and make you chuckle (I guarantee it) as you add to your knowledge. And that knowledge you get from the proven tips and cautions you will be able to use every day in the workplace.

Everybody's Got to Communicate

KING   Will you hear this letter with attention?

BIRON   As we would hear an oracle.

Love's Labour's Lost. 1, 1

Communication is a two-way (or three-way, or four-way, etc.) need. We need to hear from the king just as much as the king needs to hear from us. A fast-changing, competitive world needs timely and accurate information. Time-pressed managers increasingly rely more on meetings and presentations as key communication vehicles than on lengthy written reports as they once did in the past. Everybody is using technology such as e-mail, computer graphics, and video-conferences to expedite communication.

O, speak of that; that I do long to hear.

Claudius, King of Denmark, *Hamlet*. 2, 2

In other words, "Get me the information I need. I've got decisions to make, projects to complete, customers (and investors, and associates, and bosses) to keep happy. And I'm desperate for accurate information, sound analyses, and fast answers. In fact, I need that information for the meeting right after lunch."

Come, give us a taste of your quality; come, a
passionate speech.

Hamlet (to the Players), *Hamlet*. 2, 2

Meanwhile the process of communicating seems to take up more and more of the workplace day. The incoming e-mail list grows longer while demanding more of our attention. Meetings are the order of the day. People are hard at work preparing presentations, even from laptop computers on airplanes, and delivering them at a variety of forums. Trade magazines pile up as we desperately try to stay current but push them aside for higher priorities.

And in other areas of our lives, we're so pressed for time we depend on TV, talk radio, sound bites, and Web tips for information about how to invest, for whom to vote, and even how to get to heaven.

O, how full of briars is this working-day world!

Rosalind, *As You Like It*. 1, 3

Is This Book for You?

Do these four-centuries-old tidbits from Shakespeare actually have any application to your own world of work? I suggest the answer is . . . amazingly so. Take a look at your industry or profession, and examine what it's about. Also consider some of the common comments, frequently disparaging, about that (see the boxed text at the end of this chapter). Recall your own experiences with and impressions of other professions (or even your own):

* Science and engineering—smart but too techie and *b-o-r-i-n-g*

* Teaching—try doing that with poor communication skills

* Sales, customer service, telemarketing—Can you see much success without continuous and good communication with clients or prospects?

* Finance, investment, real estate—encumbered with jargon and paperwork

* Medical profession—flurry of complaints about the poor bedside manner of doctors and nurses

* The government—bureaucrats, forms, "not my department"

* The law—Heard any good lawyer jokes lately?

* Law enforcement—sensitive communication under tricky situations

Communication: Essential and Often Deficient

> Why, Hal, 'tis my vocation, Hal; 'tis no sin for a man
> to labour in his vocation
>
> Falstaff, *Henry IV, Part 1.* 1, 2

Falstaff was one of Shakespeare's greatest communicators. Both in his occupational pursuits and after-work activity he excelled and amply illustrated his skill at communication. His profession happened to be "purse taking."

Advance a few centuries to a classic scene from Woody Allen's *Take the Money and Run*. Woody Allen's character, Virgil Starkwell, is also engaged in purse taking, this time trying to rob a bank. Unfortunately, his poor communication capability trips him up, as the teller can't decipher Virgil's note. So he calls over the supervisor, who similarly can't figure it out. While Virgil the robber is trying to remain discreet, this miscommunication escalates up the chain of command until a whole committee is gathered around a desk trying to interpret the stickup note. If Virgil had improved his communication skills, this scene would have been over in 30 seconds, with no time-wasting committees involved at all. And he would have had the purse.

No matter what your specific discipline may be—administration, management, customer service, research, manufacturing, contracts, and so on—communication skills are needed to get the job done. How many skills are needed depends on the type of occupation involved. For some specialties, perhaps communication with a computer is all that counts. For most, however, obtaining support, being an effective team member, and getting new opportunities requires both talent and ability to communicate effectively. Doesn't it make sense to learn how to do that well?

Is there a need for good communications skills? Consider the following:

* What causes people to fail at the workplace? According to Robert Bolton in *People Skills*, 80 percent fail because they do not relate well to other people.

* In many advice columns in business journals, what seems to be the biggest concern of those asking for help? Most are

looking for answers to communication-related problems: the overdemanding boss, the inconsiderate colleague, the foul-mouthed person in the next cubicle, the slacker team member who hogs the credit, the lack of loyalty, and so on.

* In a national survey of over 1000 adults, 87 percent rated communication skills as "very important" for performing their jobs, while only 50 percent rated computer skills at the same level of importance.

* How much time of your working day do you spend in meetings? And how much of that would you say is productive? In a United Kingdom survey, nearly 25 percent of senior and middle managers said they doze off during meetings. Robert Half International, a major executive search firm, surveyed senior executives at 100 large companies. The executives reported they spent 43 percent of their time in meetings, with nearly 30 percent of that (the equivalent of six weeks per year) as wasted time. Could you use six weeks more per year for productive work?

* What about those much-maligned techies? I often hear from engineers (and I once was one) that technical knowledge is all that counts: "The data speaks for itself." *Engineering Education* magazine reported the results of a survey in which senior executives were asked about communication skills of graduate engineers. Topping the "most important" list was communication skills (writing and speaking). At the bottom of the "capability rating" list was—you guessed it— communication skills. The most important skill has the worst capability. ("Aside from the technical skills, communication skills are the most important thing you need to have," said Kathy Clark, chief executive at Landmark Systems. "So many people really underestimate those and do a bad job at them.")

Conclusion: This Book Has Something (or Plenty) for You (and Me)

Throughout this book we identify a series of key factors for communications success and apply Shakespeare's wisdom to illustrate each factor. Many of the examples are the Bard's views specifically about communication. Some are from speeches, soliloquies, and dialogues he wove into his plots. And others are his pithy lines that may not have pertained to communications per se but fit so well to the communications topic that I've adapted them to make a point.

Shakespeare's works mix heavy drama, rich language, outrageous situations, and low comedy. I'll apply that same methodology to this book. Whatever your level of communication background, skill, or need, you'll find that his words, insights, insults, and quips can tweak your interest and add to your personal toolkit. By following *Say It Like Shakespeare*, you, too, can become an effective communicator.

> Whose words all ears took captive.
>
> Lafeu, *All's Well That Ends Well.* 5, 3

Take-Away Ideas

* Communication is hugely important in the workplace.
* The need for better communication is also huge.
* The Bard's many insights can help you sharpen your own communication skills.

POLITICIANS	Get thee glass eyes, And, like a scurvy politician, seem To see the things thou dost not. Lear, *King Lear*. 4, 6
CONTRACTS	I like not fair terms and a villain's mind. Bassanio, *The Merchant of Venice*. 1, 3
ENGINEERS	For 'tis the sport to have the engineer Hoist with his own petard. Hamlet, *Hamlet*. 3, 4
LEADERS	Uneasy lies the head that wears a crown. Henry, IV, *Henry IV, Part 2*. 3, 1
PREACHERS	I tell thee, churlish priest, A ministering angel shall my sister be, When thou liest howling. Hamlet, *Hamlet*. 5, 1
LAWYERS	Why may not that be the skull of a lawyer? Where be his quiddities now, his quills, his cases, his tenures, and his tricks? Hamlet, *Hamlet*. 5, 1
JUDGES	See how yon justice rails upon yon simple thief. Hark in thine ear: change places and handy-dandy, which is the justice, which is the thief? Lear, *King Lear*. 4, 6
JURY MEMBERS	The jury, passing on the prisoner's life May in the sworn twelve have a thief or two Guiltier than him they try. Angelo, *Measure for Measure*. 2, 1

PHYSICIANS	Trust not the physician; His antidotes are poison, and he slays More than you rob. <div align="right">Timon, *Timon of Athens.* 4, 3</div>
PHILOSOPHERS	Preach some philosophy to make me mad. <div align="right">Constance, *King John.* 3, 4</div>

Chapter 2

Exceeding Wise or Counterfeit Rascal: What's Your Personal Scorecard?

He was indeed the glass
Wherein the noble youth did dress themselves.

Lady Percy, *Henry IV, Part 2*. 2, 3

Now let's get you started on your path to upgraded communications capability. With the Bard's help, we'll suggest some standards for good and poor communication and ways to size up your own needs.

What Does Good Communication Mean?

Both during my corporate career and as an independent consultant, I've been privileged to have worked with many leaders and team members. It usually takes about a day and one or two meetings to sense the camaraderie of the team, which mostly reflects the style of the leader. If the team members are good communicators, the environment is less tense, the up and down flow is freer, and the mutual support and respect come through clearly.

[We] observed his courtship to the common people;
How he did seem to dive into their hearts
With humble and familiar courtesy;
What reverence he did throw away on slaves,
Wooing poor craftsmen with the craft of smiles . . .

Richard II, *Richard II*. 1, 4

O now, who will behold
The royal captain of this ruined band
Walking from watch to watch, from tent to tent,
Let him cry "Praise and glory on his head!"
For forth he goes and visits all his host,
Bids them good morrow with a modest smile,
And calls them brothers, friends, and countrymen . . .
That every wretch, pining and pale before,
Beholding him, plucks comfort from his looks.

Chorus, *Henry V*. 4, prologue

In your working world, do you have much trouble recognizing a good communicator, a good leader? We tend to make these our role models, and use their manner, style, and techniques as attributes to emulate. Have you seen any difference in your own or the troops' willingness to work with good as opposed to poor communicators? How strong is the loyalty, trust, openness, zest, camaraderie, and motivation? There is often a direct correlation.

Marlin Fitzwater in *Call the Briefing*, sized up his boss, President George Bush: "By the time Larry Speaks resigned from the White House in 1987, I had developed an enormous loyalty to the Bush family. The vice president and Mrs. Bush had a knack for making the staff feel wanted and appreciated. He was master of the small gesture that made a big difference: the arm around the shoulder after you had made a mistake, the signed photograph when you needed to feel important, the private dinner when you felt left out, and, most remarkably, the ability to recognize the everyday problems of staff frictions and competitions."

What About Not So Good Communication?

> His forward voice, now, is to speak well of his friend; his
> backward voice is to utter foul speeches and to detract.
>
> Stephan, *The Tempest.* 2, 2

Shakespeare was especially good at coming up with juicy descriptions that captured the nature of scoundrels. As you read these, do any names or faces come to mind?

> Why this is an arrant counterfeit rascal; I remember him
> now; a bawd, a cutpurse.
>
> Gower, *Henry V.* 3, 6

> It is not enough to speak, but to speak true.
>
> Lysander, *A Midsummer Night's Dream.* 5, 1

> O, where is faith? O, where is loyalty?
>
> Henry VI, *Henry VI, Part 2.* 5, 1

> Is there no respect of place, persons, nor time in you?
>
> Malvolio, *Twelfth Night.* 2, 3

> But man, proud man, Dressed in a little brief author-
> ity . . .
>
> Isabella, *Measure for Measure.* 2, 2

> For new-made honour doth forget men's names.
>
> Philip the Bastard, *King John.* 1, 1

Those all are old, Shakespearean-era, sixteenth-century styles of communicating. Would these fit the modern world? Here are some comments from present-day employees rating their own chief top executives. Note the similarity with the Bard's pack.

* "Ruthless, crude, arbitrary whip-cracker who deliberately made employees paranoid."

* "Berated senior executives in front of their own subordinates."

* "A master of confrontation who conducts meetings with a verbal cattle prod."

* "Once threatened to kick security analyst in the groin for interrupting him."

* "Couldn't stand it when someone disagreed with him, even in private. He'd eat you alive, calling you a dumb SOB."

* "Accomplished at belittling employees in front of others."

Again, imagine the attitude of the troops when working with such people, whether they are bosses, colleagues, customers, or subordinates. Would they engender loyalty? Trust? Support? Enjoyment? Commitment? Is there a price to be paid for poor communication? Whether a manager or not, a poor communicator can pollute the team spirit and hamper success.

Marlin Fitzwater sized up another of his bosses, John Sununu, chief of staff: "He is a nerd, and nurtures his reputation for brilliance. In college he was the one with a slide rule. In the White House he carried computer games around. . . . But there were flaws. His loyalty had a price: power. His intelligence had a blind spot: arrogance. After a few months as chief of staff it was clear that one day his enemies would reach up and devour him. He was adding enemies daily. . . .

As he offended one person after another in Washington with his bellicose personality and belligerent meetings, his pack of defenders grew smaller."

Are You Talking to Me?

Men's faults do seldom to themselves appear.

The Rape of Lucrece

"All well and good," you may be saying, "but what are you talking to me for? I've been communicating since I was a babe. I can talk as well as anybody. Heck, I'm always the life of the party."

The fool doth think he is wise, but the wise man
knows himself to be a fool.

Touchstone, *As You Like It.* 5, 1

I've conducted hundreds of communication seminars and classes, and I generally find that the attendees most receptive to learning are already reasonably good communicators. "More, more, I want to get better." The clearly marginal communicators are the ones who, at the start of the classes, are most likely to sit in defensive postures, show expressions of disinterest, and barely participate. "How long will this last? We've got more important things to do."

Many a time and often I ha' dined with him, and told
him on't . . . and yet he would embrace no counsel,
take no warning.

Lucullus, *Timon of Athens.* 3, 1

As a frequent coach of high-stakes teams, I have seen a pattern in which a team whose leader is a good communicator tends to embrace fresh approaches and feedback. Teams led by weak communicators are frequently tougher to help, and they need help the most.

In *In Search of Excellence*, Tom Peters and Robert Waterman write, "The nature and uses of communication in the excellent companies are remarkably different from those of their nonexcellent peers. The excellent companies are a vast network of informal, open communications. . . . The intensity of communications is unmistakable."

Get a Report Card

He was a scholar, and a ripe and good one;
Exceeding wise, fair-spoken and persuading.

Griffith, *Henry VIII*. 4, 2

By asking others, such as your supervisor and colleagues, you may find out what your communication strengths and weaknesses are. Keep this exercise productive by getting feedback about your positive as well as negative attributes to head off a finger-pointing, sniping process. If you are a supervisor, take a look at 360° feedback and upward evaluation, concepts widely used today. Done right, these provide feedback about how fellow employees—up, down, and across—rate you.

So shall inferior eyes,
That borrow their behaviours from the great,
Grow great by your example, and put on
The dauntless spirit of resolution.

Philip the Bastard, *King John*. 5, 1

Sounds good so far. He's clearly an astute observer, in spite of his shaky parentage.

> With that, all laugh'd, and clapped him on the
> shoulder,
> Making the bold wag by their praises bolder.
> One rubb'd his elbow thus, and fleer'd, and swore
> A better speech was never spoke before.
>
> Boyet, *Love's Labour's Lost.* 5, 2

Well, boss, if I'm really coming across that well, how about that raise we've been discussing for some time? And those stock options?

> . . . his undressed, unpolished, uneducated, unpruned,
> untrained, or, rather, unlettered, or, ratherest,
> unconfirmed fashion.
>
> Holofernes, *Loves' Labour's Lost.* 4, 2

So, boss, what do you really think about me?

> You speak like a green girl,
> Unsifted in such perilous circumstance.
>
> Polonius, *Hamlet.* 1, 3

Thanks a lot! Didn't your mother tell you if you have nothing good to say about someone, don't say anything? Or are you sending me a message that I would be wise to heed? Could I have a second opinion?

> Ay, that's a colt indeed, for he doth talk nothing but
> talk of his horse.
>
> Portia, *The Merchant of Venice.* 1, 2

Now how 'bout them Cubs/Chargers/Knicks?

In case the personal input seemed to come through your rose-colored glasses, attending a seminar or class—especially a participatory one—can quickly bring to the surface flaws you didn't realize you had. Many organizations provide access to personal coaches for one-on-one tweaking. Video review, especially with a knowledgeable coach, can be a big help in identifying areas for correction. One fellow was reviewing a tape of himself following a practice presentation. "I'm so boring I can hardly stay awake," he moaned. How do you think his listeners felt?

If confidants will give you honest feedback, in a tactful way, and you are able to receive and process it without treating it lightly ("Oh, you're exaggerating,"), reacting defensively ("Oh, yeah? You ain't so perfect yourself!"), or even responding in a hostile manner ("Stick it in your ear, Charlie! I'm outta here!"), this can provide valuable information as a starting place for improvement.

Walk the Talk?

> But, good my brother,
> Do not, as some ungracious pastors do,
> Show me the steep and thorny way to heaven,
> Whilest, like a puff'd and reckless libertine,
> Himself the primrose path of dalliance treads
> And recks not his own rede.
>
> Ophelia, *Hamlet.* 1, 3

Ophelia reminds her lecturing brother not to talk one thing and do the opposite. Do any real names and faces come to mind—say in the world of politics or religion—as example of talking a good practice while pursuing the opposite path?

Even better than a seminar or a coach may be the role model. Employees pay close attention to the examples they see from colleagues they respect, immediate supervisors and senior management.

In many training sessions when I observe poor practices and suggest better ways, the response often is "But I do it the same way my boss does" or "I agree with you, but I know if I tried it the boss wouldn't let me do it."

My views on running meetings were shaped during several years of program reviews during the early days of the space program. Meetings occurred on a regular basis and involved multiple contractors and government agencies. The levels of efficiency, enjoyment, and success were very different depending on the person in charge. I tried to conduct my own smaller meetings applying the same techniques as the one whose style got better results.

As a seminar leader, I learned early the importance of getting bosses in on the process, by either having them participate in the same educational program as their employees or clearly supporting our goals and methods. For a series of presentation training seminars at Northrop Grumman, the top vice president sponsoring the programs went through the program and got his plaudits and suggestions just like everybody else. And he insisted that those reporting directly to him also go through it (I'd bet with some grumbling). That conveyed a strong message to the other attendees: This is serious, he believes it, and he expects us to try it.

Ken Blanchard, Chief Spiritual Officer (I'm not kidding) of his own consulting firm and author of *The One Minute Manager*, said he's been asked by some city governments to train staff, but not those at the top. He says, "You can't get them to come," so he has declined. "A fish stinks from the head down," he says, "so that's where you start. If the people at the top aren't with it, they can sabotage anything."

The price of a "Do as I say, not as I do" approach is loss of credibility and nonacceptance. Ask any teenager whose father warns him to stay away from drugs while working his way through a six-pack.

Take-Away Ideas

* Set your own measures of good and poor communicators.
* Either from self-assessment or from others, identify your own strengths and improvement needs.
* To be effective with others, be a good role model.
* Improving communication involves many aspects.

Chapter 3

❦

Mend Your Speech a Little: Ready to Go?

You may have a long pattern of good intentions. You may even have thought about digging deeper into communication than your *Dilbert* calender. But you passed when the company offered a seminar on listening, then one on better writing, and one on presentations, and one on conflict management. So with the Bard's help let's see if we can start that spark toward making it happen. We'll also establish a communication model that will help us stay on course in the chapters that follow.

Time for Communication Update?

> How now, Cordelia! Mend your speech a little,
> Lest it may mar your fortunes.
>
> Lear, *King Lear*. 1, 1

As is often the case with advice from parents, the child didn't take it and, sure enough, her fortune was marred. "Mending speech," or becoming proficient at communicating, is one of the key factors in achieving success in many enterprises today.

If this news be true,
Poor queen and son, your labour is but lost;
For Warwick is a subtle orator,
And Lewis a prince soon won with moving words.

Henry VI, Henry VI, Part 3. 3, 1

Take a look around. What about the colleagues (a.k.a. competitors) with whom you're vying for promotion or better opportunities? What if they're strong communicators and you're just average, or worse?

Turn him to any cause of policy,
The Gordian knot of it he will unloose,
Familiar as his garter: that, when he speaks,
The air, a charter'd libertine, is still,
And the mute wonder lurketh in men's ears,
To steal his sweet and honey'd sentences.

Canterbury, Henry V. 1, 1

Let's hope this spellbinder is on *your* team, not the competition's. You've seen powerful communicators at work and in life. They're the ones who are able to bring conflicting factions together on a common course, who can win over customers and bring in contracts, who can add pride and teamwork to a lethargic or disgruntled work force. They're the ones likely to get the raises or the next openings, aren't they?

BUCKINGHAM   Now, my lord, what shall we do, if we
        perceive Lord Hastings will not yield to our complots?

GLOUCESTER   Chop off his head, man.

Richard III. 3, 1

Perhaps this more resembles your style of communication. It does have the advantage of swiftly, and cleanly, eliminating those who disagree with you. But that may not be the most effective approach in today's business world.

> Hold, as 'twere, the mirror up to nature; to show virtue
> her own feature, scorn her own image.
>
> Hamlet (to the Players), *Hamlet*. 3, 2

This is the painful part—taking that look in the mirror to see if just possibly *you*, as distinct from that other person you know that we've been talking about, have one or two communication areas on which you might not score so well. Even I hear regularly (from family, friends, associates, waiters, strangers, the dogs, etc.) when one of my well-intended communications misfires. It's hard to find a perfect communicator, so where do your tiny imperfections lie that might be revealed—and, more important, corrected—with introspection?

Ready to Start?

> I would I had bestowed that time in the tongues that I
> have in fencing, dancing, and bear-baiting. O, had I
> but followed the arts!
>
> Aguecheek, *Twelfth Night*. 1, 3

It's one thing to have knowledge and capability; it's another to be able to communicate well with colleagues, upper management, customers, and the public. Communication skills are the key to winning over audiences in many forums: business, sales, finance, community organizations, religion, and politics. Many people achieve advancement and success because of communication proficiency; others are held back through lack of it. Which camp would you rather be in?

There is a tide in the affairs of men
Which taken at the flood leads on to fortune;
Omitted, all the voyage of their life
Is bound in shallows and in miseries.
On such a full sea we are now afloat,
And we must take the current when it serves,
Or lose our ventures.

Brutus, *Julius Caesar.* 4, 3

Now, despite the fact that Brutus and his associates did "take the current" and paid a heavy price for it, since they lost, is the point not still valid? If you accept that being successful in your enterprise is linked with the ability to communicate well, doesn't it then follow that you'll add to your success by taking the "better communications current"?

Where's That Remedy?

Our remedies oft in ourselves do lie,
Which we ascribe to heaven.

Helena, *All's Well That Ends Well.* 1, 1

So what will you do about it? If you're like a large part of the assemblage of people I've met, in business and elsewhere, over the years, the answer is probably "not much."

In asked dozens of seminars and college classes, I've asked attendees how many own a single book on interpersonal communication, better meetings, or dealing with conflict. Few hands go up. "How many are Toastmasters?" Maybe one or two hands go up. Yet most reply, "Yes, I know I should do something to become a better communicator."

Men at some time are masters of their fates:
The fault, dear Brutus, is not in our stars,
but in ourselves . . .

Cassius, *Julius Caesar.* 1, 2

It's one thing to wish you were a better communicator, and another
to set a plan in gear to actually achieve that. Perhaps you'd like to
become a better speaker. You know it's important. You've seen those
glazed eyes in the audience sitting around the conference table. Your
boss has hinted that your speaking skills need some serious attention.
But you hesitate. You say, "Good idea, maybe later."

I've seen the fingernail tracks in the training room carpet from
people who've had to be dragged into a seminar. They were carrying
heavy anxiety, discomfort about training, and a batch of excuses.
Invariably, once on board and participating, they've become enthu-
siastic participants.

Enough Ducking

Our doubts are traitors,
And make us lose the good we oft might win
By fearing to attempt.

Lucio, *Measure for Measure.* 1, 4

Do you have some resistance to this communication stuff? Do you
think it would be too pushy to chair a meeting? Do you doubt that
you have anything of value to offer by speaking up? Do the butterflies
start to flutter at the thought? Do you feel that you don't want to
brag, or mess up? Would you prefer that someone else take the
spotlight?

Well, forget all that! Let's review the old attitudes that have kept
you in a comfort zone of little risk. It's time to stretch, to stop

 27

ducking the possibilities that come your way, and to seek out ways to spotlight your capability.

> Experience is by industry achieved,
> And perfected by the swift course of time.
>
> Antonio, *The Two Gentlemen of Verona*. 1, 3

Perhaps you're reluctant to work on the communication aspect of your professional growth because you still carry the memory of past setbacks. Maybe you goofed up in the church Christmas pageant and your pals laughed at you. You dreaded the mandatory public speaking course in college. (I wasn't thrilled by it either, but I had the perfect excuse: I was an engineer.) You started to make a comment in a meeting but garbled it.

Maybe you carry the need for perfection, often associated with professional disciplines (e.g., the necessity for scientific or medical reports to be error-free). Trying and missing leads to resistance against trying again. Communication is far from a perfect science, or art.

Where Are You Headed?

> Lord, we know what we are, but know not what we
> may be.
>
> Ophelia, *Hamlet*. 4, 5

Another argument I often hear is "I see no need for all this added training. In my job we don't do any fancy communicating. My skills are perfectly adequate for what I need to do." This ignores some pertinent issues:

* What do you want to be doing in one, five, or ten years?
* What communication skills will that role demand?
* What are your chances of getting that desired assignment with only "adequate" communication skills?

> Who seeks, and will not take when once 'tis offer'd,
> Shall never find it more.
>
> Menas, *Antony and Cleopatra.* 2, 7

So this could be opportunity calling. Are you answering?

Blow That Trumpet

> Therefore it is most expedient for the wise . . . to be
> trumpet of his own virtues.
>
> Benedick, *Much Ado About Nothing.* 5, 2

You've probably noticed that those who get ahead are generally not the shy, retiring types. When upper managers review candidates for new opportunities, they consider several factors. One is competence to do the expanded tasks the new job requires; many of those, such as becoming a group supervisor, leading a project team, and moving into customer service, will require increased communication activity. What better way to be considered than to communicate well when those opportunities arise, or even to seek some out if they don't—to start "blowing your own trumpet"?

Another bard often quoted, Ralph Waldo Emerson, wrote, "Build a better mouse trap and the world will beat a path to your door." Unfortunately that is mostly myth. A lot of people with good skills have found that the world is ignoring them. I've concluded that the only time the world will beat that path without your trumpet blaring is when you're in the bathroom at a large meeting with limited facilities.

Can't Teach an Old Horse?

> Sir, I am too old to learn.
>
> Kent, Othello. 2, 2

I've heard these excuses many times: "I'm too set in my ways." "It's too hard to change old habits." "If it ain't broke, don't fix it." These are the real messages behind such statements: "I'm really too lazy to put forth the effort." "I don't think it's worth the trouble." "You're taking me out of my comfort zone."

> Happy in this, she is not yet so old
> But she may learn.
>
> Portia, The Merchant of Venice. 3, 2

People in business know they have to keep up with progress or they'll be left behind. When I started my engineering career, everybody used slide rules. Then simple electronic calculators came along (it was a huge breakthrough when a colleague showed up with one that could do square roots!). Now the person next to me on the plane is checking e-mail from a wallet-sized wireless gadget. The senior associates become just as proficient, within limits, about the tools and processes of their trade as the new hires. Why does the same not hold true for the soft skills, such as learning how to interact better with colleagues or customers?

The Rewards Are Waiting

Bell, book and candle shall not drive me back,
When gold and silver becks me to come on.

Philip the Bastard, *King John*. 3, 3

In case you are "fearing to attempt" or still need motivation, consider these dauntless words of the Bastard (no comparison intended). When the reward was clear and valuable ("gold and silver"), he would not be deterred by obstacles and threats ("candle," meaning excommunication, was pretty serious). Look forward to either your immediate or long-term goal, and assess whether you're likely to achieve it with mediocre communications capability.

Bill Walton today is recognized as a highly talented TV sports commentator. Was he some sort of natural communicator? Far from it, as he tells in his autobiography. He was a terrible communicator— so bad that the idea of becoming an announcer when he retired from his professional basketball career was ludicrous. He decided to address the problem, and we regularly see the result of his adding communication skills to his background (and he collects the reward).

To business that we love we rise betime,
And go to 't with delight.

Antony, *Antony and Cleopatra*. 4, 4

Sharan Wendel is an electrical engineering graduate from the University of South Florida. She advanced rapidly in her career to Vice President of Technology & Logistics for nChip, Inc. in Silicon Valley. "There were a lot of technically competent engineers around me, many smarter than I," she said. "The key to my success was communications, people skills, and presentation skills. Most engineers don't have these, so that made me stand out from my colleagues."

She retired at the age of 37 ("My goal was 40") and with her husband bought a luxury recreational vehicle resort in Northern California. Then they received recognition as the top California RV resort for three years, and the top national resort for two years. "It comes back once more to communication—you have to have a good product and market yourself."

Our Communication Model

What follows are specific chapters dealing with the various parts of communication. The lines are not as clean as they appear to be in the illustration below, as the roles of sender and receiver are constantly shifting:

In helping you tune all the parts, we'll review the factors associated with

* *Sender*: Attitude, voice, language, appearance, nonverbal communication, mental preparation
* *Receiver*: Listening, questioning, critical evaluation
* *Feedback*: Role switching as receivers become senders, and senders listeners
* *Message*: Communication assessment, strategy, organization, reinforcement
* *Medium*: Methodology of communication, computers, graphics, props, projectors, arrangements, preparation

Take-Away Ideas:

* Communication is important for success in business and life.

* Key to positive change is commitment to review and action.

* Blow that trumpet, and keep applying the lessons learned.

* Be ready to reap the rewards that come with better communication.

Part II

The Sender's Role

Macbeth. 3, 4

Over the next five chapters we focus on the sender's role in the communication process: voice, words, body language, wardrobe, mental readiness.

Chapter 4

Speak the Speech, Trippingly: Tune Up That Voice

> Speak the speech, I pray you, as I pronounced it to
> you, trippingly on the tongue. But if you mouth it,
> as many of your players do, I had as lief the
> towncrier spoke my lines.
>
> Hamlet (to the Players), *Hamlet.* 3, 2

What good is a well-crafted message if it is delivered in a monotone that puts the audience to sleep, or in a whining style that makes listeners cringe? How does your voice rate? Is it helping you communicate, or does it have characteristics that are hampering your success? Here we'll look at some of the keys to vocal power, primarily from the sender perspective.

In spoken communication your voice is a key factor in how well your audience attends to you and your message. We react differently to voices that are pleasant versus those that are irritating, to those that are forceful versus timid, and to those that are smooth versus stumbling.

Is Your Voice Appealing?

What is't thou say'st? Her voice was ever soft,
Gentle and low, an excellent thing in woman.

Lear, *King Lear*. 5, 3

What do you notice first about a voice? Typically, our first reaction is to its quality. If it is pleasing, firm, or dramatic we tend to listen and keep listening. Mention names of certain public figures, and the quality of their voices come to mind. James Earl Jones: "This is CNN," or that menacing voice of Darth Vader. (During the 2000 Sydney Olympics opening ceremonies, Jones' voice was heard during one early segment. Said Bob Costas, "I guess you could say it's an announcer's nightmare to follow the voice of James Earl Jones."

Oprah Winfrey has had amazing success on TV, for a variety of reasons. I suggest that her strong, forceful voice is a key factor, and that if her voice were thin or shrill she would not be at the top of her profession. And who does not recognize in a flash the voice of Paul Harvey when it comes on the radio?

. . . once I sat upon a promontory
And heard a mermaid, on a dolphin's back,
Uttering such dulcet and harmonious breath,
That the rude sea grew civil at her song,
And certain stars shot madly from their spheres . . .

Oberon, *A Midsummer Night's Dream*. 2, 1

Voices of pleasant nature, spoken or sung, can definitely affect our mood, spirit, and receptivity.

A melodious, voice and flowing speech pattern are valuable attributes for lovers, public speakers, aspirants to high office, and anyone else who has a message to get across. A special or distinctive local quality has an immediate and lasting impact. For example, when you hear these names, do you recall their memorable voices? Rod Serling, Walter Cronkite, Kathleen Turner, Vin Scully.

Other voices may not be regarded as ideal, but they have an unforgettable quality that works for them. Think of Howard Cosell, Clint Eastwood, Barbara Mikulski, Jack Nicholson, Rosie Perez, and Public Radio's Click and Clack.

Are You Projecting?

I will aggravate my voice so, that I will roar you as
gently as any sucking dove; I will roar you an 'twere
any nightingale.

Bottom, *A Midsummer Night's Dream.* 1, 2

Adequate projection is important, especially in group situations. If you can't be heard, you're likely to be squelched by someone with a stronger voice. In meetings when people are introducing themselves or making statements, quite often their voices are so thin people will shout "Speak up!" or "Use a mic!" or will just ignore the information. Another common situation occurs during a discussion when those seated in the back can't hear the conversation of those in front, with the repeated appeal "Can't hear you! . . . Please repeat the question!" Many current RFPs (requests for proposal) state that reviewers will ask no questions *unless the speaker cannot be heard.*

Tip: Be sensitive to weak projection, and consciously send your voice out to the person seated farthest away in the room.

Thou but offend'st thy lungs to speak so loud.

Shylock, *The Merchant of Venice.* 4, 1

Also make sure you're not belting it out too strong. A thundering voice can generate a strong desire in listeners to depart.

Or Are You Howling? Whining? Grating?

> An had he had been a dog that should have howled
>   thus, they would have hanged him; and I pray God
>   his bad voice bode no mischief. I had as lief have
>   heard the night-raven, come what plague could have
>   come after it.
>
> Benedick, *Much Ado About Nothing*. 2, 3

Comics use their voices to make us laugh. Don Knotts, Phyllis Diller, Rosanne, Jonathan Winters, the entire Simpson family, and Bullwinkle's Natasha and Boris all have exaggerated vocal qualities as part of their characters.

Do the voices of these people cause any reaction? Henry Kissinger, Ross Perot, Julia Child, Richard Simmons. When not intentionally fudged, voices of shaky quality can lead us to

* Be amused and poke fun at the voice (usually behind the speaker's back).

* Be irritated by shrieking, guttural, whiny, or nasal voices much as by fingernails scratching a blackboard.

* Miss the words because the vocal distraction overwhelms the message.

* Discontinue the dialogue or relationship.

* Vote against the candidate whose voice irritates us and vote for the one whose voice doesn't.

Voice coach Jeffrey Jacobi conducted a survey to find out which voices Americans find most annoying. Forty-four percent said whining, nagging voices; 16 percent said high-pitched and squeaky voices; 12 percent said loud, grating speech; also-rans were mumblers, very fast talkers, and monotonous voices.

Trippingly Off the Tongue, or Murdering Thy Breath?

Murder thy breath in middle of a word,
And then begin again, and stop again,
As if thou wert distraught and mad with terror?

Gloucester, *Richard III*. 3, 5

Slushmouth English is my term for diction that leads to several reactions, all damaging to the speaker: (1) you don't understand it, (2) you are distracted from the message, and (3) you subconsciously or consciously make a judgment that the person's sloppy diction indicates a sloppy mind or lack of polish.

Examples of these kinds of voices can be heard every day on your phone answering machine. They're the ones whose messages you have to play over several times, and then you still can't figure out who called, what their message was, and what the callback number is. The message from a clear speaker is slowly and clearly stated: "This is Joe Smith, J-o-e S-m-i-t-h, Joe Smith. Smith, as in blacksmith. Just called to say hello." The message from a mushy or auctioneer-type speaker sounds like this: "PROBLEM!!! Thz Hlenzimenneq Razzaeembeplbbble.Nummr 6zippppp. IMPORTANT!!" When will they catch on that it makes sense to speak such messages slowly and distinctly, and then repeat the key information?

The head of the Central Intelligence Agency during the Iran-Contra investigations was William Casey. In *Veil*, Bob Woodward wrote, "[Casey] went to the Senate Intelligence Committee's secure hearing room and sat at the long witness table where a special microphone stood like a praying mantis poking in his face. It was to aid the senators in deciphering the Director's legendary mumbling."

Vocal distractions can quickly and seriously raise the receptor's hackles. "They, uh, uh, I mean, y'know speak like, uh, stum, stumblingly, not, like, you know trippingly." (These are the ones who drive Toastmasters up the wall fast.)

Actor Anthony Quinn, born in Mexico, didn't learn to speak English until he was 12. As a young man he showed talent in art and won an architectural competition. This led to a meeting with Frank Lloyd Wright, who asked Quinn what he wanted to do. Quinn said he mumbled and stumbled so badly that Wright said he'd never make it unless he learned to speak more clearly. So he became an actor. Go figure.

What about accents? They can add character, value, and charm if the speaker can be easily understood. Why should Sophia Loren, Charles Aznavour, and Desmond Tutu change their accents? If they can't be understood, that's a different story, whether native English speakers or not. I once conducted a presentations training seminar for a large corporation. Several of the participants were good presenters, but difficult to understand. Following my suggestion, the company brought in a voice coach who worked with the people over several weeks. The improvement was obvious and valuable back on the job.

What Does Your Voice Reveal?

> Methinks thy voice is alter'd and thou speak'st
> In better phrase and matter than thou didst.

Gloucester, King Lear. 4, 6

If you're not excited about your proposition, why should others be? A lackluster delivery stirs few crowds; one inspired by passion is likely to command more attention. A monotone delivery style, also extremely common, can put us to sleep, which is why hypnotists use the technique intentionally.

Voices can reveal. They can carry more message than just words. When a friend is sick or depressed, can't you detect it from the voice, even without seeing him or her? Similarly, an upbeat voice connotes a positive, cheerful person. So before you make that important phone call, consider the effect your mood has on your voice and the impression that it will instantly create.

> I would have such a fellow whipped for o'erdoing
> Termagant. It out-Herods Herod: pray you, avoid it.
>
> Hamlet (to the Players), *Hamlet. 3, 2*

There is an old tale of a preacher delivering his sermon. He followed along with his written script and noted the handwritten note to himself beside one paragraph: "Weak point. Shout!" We're in an era of talk radio and confrontational TV where the secret to success seems to be to outshout the other person. Forget about logic, courtesy, and willingness to listen to another point of view; just shout louder than the other person.

Voice Is Only Part of the Story

> She that was ever fair and never proud,
> Had tongue at will, and yet was never loud.
>
> Iago, *Othello. 2, 1*

Eleanor Roosevelt had a thin, high-pitched voice, not at all a rich timbre. For several decades, she was a prominent speaker on radio and television, and her voice was immediately recognized. In spite of her vocal limitations, she had a significant effect on many issues.

Thomas Dewey had a successful political career in New York and then ran for president. His voice was the richest of any public figure's, but not enough to pull him into the presidency he was expected to win, in 1948, versus somewhat scratchy-voiced Harry Truman.

Perking Up Your Voice

> For my voice, I have lost it with halloing and singing of anthems.
>
> Falstaff, *Henry IV, Part 2.* 1, 2

Did you ever lose your voice, such as after the big game? Maybe an illness left you with a weak voice or even laryngitis. If you're a long-time smoker, you probably have vocal roughness and the wonderful hacking that goes with the habit. (Shakespeare fans may cast a jaundiced eye at Falstaff's excuse, as he was rarely found anywhere near a church, unless to dip into the collection plate.)

Actually, the ones who rarely have vocal trouble are those who appear regularly in the choir or barbershop quartet. Singing has long been recommended as a way to maintain vocal quality. Reading aloud every day, especially poetry and stories, helps improve smoothness and inflection. In coaching speakers with obvious vocal quality problems, I've observed two standard characteristics: They rarely sing, even in the shower, or they are smokers.

> The preyful princess pierced and pricked a pretty pleasing pricket . . .
>
> Holofernes, *Love's Labour's Lost.* 4, 2

Reading tongue twisters aloud can help improve vocal fluency and clarity. Say "toy boat" many times quickly. At first you probably won't get past two or three times; with practice you can get up to ten. Got that mastered? Try "sizzling swizzle stick" or even "nattering nabobs of negativism." Mannerisms such as too many "uhs" or "y'knows" can be identified by having a colleague count them, or by listening to an audiotape of yourself and then personal coaching or joining a Toastmasters Club. Compensation for an accent or correction for improper use of the voice may require a speech or voice coach, as these are difficult to self-diagnose and correct. This can be a worthwhile investment.

Take-Away Ideas

* A voice of good caliber can be a valuable asset in business communication.

* Your opportunities and success may be set back by poor vocal qualities.

* As with any valuable asset, training and care of your voice is important.

* If you know your voice is a problem, invest in professional help.

Chapter 5

Speak Plain and to the Purpose: Enhancing Language Power

This royal throne of kings, this sceptred isle,
This earth of majesty, this seat of Mars,
This other Eden, demi-paradise;
This fortress built by Nature for herself
Against infection and the hand of war;
This happy breed of men, this little world,
This precious stone set in the silver sea,
Which serves it in the office of a wall
Or as a moat defensive to a house,
Against the envy of less happier lands;
This blessed plot, this earth, this realm, this England.

John of Gaunt, *King Richard II.* 2, 1

Whew! The man did have a way with words. I recall seeing Basil Rathbone, as Sherlock Holmes, recite these words during the closing scene of one of the master detective's mysteries. Holmes was gazing seaward from the white cliffs while stirring music played in the background and the flag waved in the stiff breeze. It took a herculean effort to keep from rising from my easy chair to stand and break into

↝␥ 47 ␦↜

"God Save the Queen" while tears of pride welled up in my eyes. And I'm not even British.

In this chapter we'll look at ways that your language—words and phrases—can add to the power of communication. In the next chapter, with help from the Bard's examples, we'll see how language flaws can take away from that power.

Good Words Can Have Lasting Power

Whate'er you think, good words, I think, were best.

Philip the Bastard, *King John*. 4, 3

Many of Shakespeare's lines, written long ago, are ingrained into the language we use today. The enormous output of his writings and the haste with which many were produced have made audiences marvel at his power. Here are some examples in which you'll have no trouble catching the memorable words.

And Caesar's spirit ranging for revenge,
With Ate by his side come hot from hell,
Shall in these confines with a monarch's voice
Cry "Havoc," and let slip the dogs of war

Antony, *Julius Caesar*. 3, 1

When to the sessions of sweet silent thought
I summon up remembrance of things past . . .

Sonnet 30

What a piece of work is a man! How noble in reason!
How infinite in faculty! In form and moving how
express and admirable! In action how like an angel!

Hamlet, *Hamlet*. 2, 2

Do Your Words Bring Listeners to Their Knees?

> I am vanquished; these haughty words of hers
> Have batter'd me like roaring cannon-shot,
> And made me almost yield upon my knees.
>
> Burgundy, after a speech by Pucelle (Joan of Arc),
> *Henry VI, Part 1. 3, 3*

There is ample evidence that language has the power to affect audiences positively. From the early Greeks we have not only the example of the power of great orators, such as Demosthenes, but also the methods, spelled out especially by Aristotle, that communicators can use to apply language to achieve their ends, hopefully noble. Many of the major events of history can trace their inspiration or instigation to the power of language.

> 'Tis but a peevish boy; yet he talks well;
> But what care I for words? Yet words do well
> When he that speaks them pleases those that hear.
>
> Phebe, *As You Like It. 3, 5*

Who come to mind as people whose masterful language stirred audiences at the time and are still quoted perhaps centuries later? Pick your field—communicators have made lasting impressions via the spoken or written word. Let me suggest a few; you fill in the words

* *Conquest.* Julius Caesar: "I came, I saw, I _____" (or, for the Latin students, "Veni, vidi, vici,").

* *Revolution.* "Liberté, Egalité, _____."

* *Statesmanship.* Franklin Delano Roosevelt: "We have nothing to fear but _____."

* *Movies*. Mae West: "Come up and _____."
* *Sports*. Muhammed Ali: "Float like a butterfly, _____."
* *Politics*. Ross Perot: "That incredible _____ sound."

Are Your Words Telling Your Tale Plainly?

An honest tale speeds best being plainly told.

Queen Elizabeth, *Richard III*. 4, 4

If you have a message to convey, check your words to see how many can be replaced with better choices or cut entirely. For example, try to rephrase the following: "A member of the nonfemale species inclined toward prevarication, even internalizing in excess, fundamentally for the most part will almost always fail to emerge victorious." It takes some work, to interpret, but that is the same as "He who hesitates is lost." Want some other examples? Read the instructions from the Internal Revenue Service, or your Living Trust, or the thick stack of documents you signed when you bought your house.

He was wont to speak plain and to the purpose.

Benedick, *Much Ado About Nothing*. 2, 3

A classic focused statement was the response during the Battle of the Bulge in World War II by General Anthony McAuliffe. To the German demand that he surrender, he replied, "Nuts!"

He had some historical precedent from the Spartans (think Kirk Douglas), from the state of Laconia in ancient Greece. When Philip of Macedon wrote, "If I enter Laconia, I will level Sparta to the ground," the Spartan response was "If."

I suspect you will recall these phrases, all plain but powerful in capturing a message. Who said them?

From history:
* ✳ "Go west, young man."
* ✳ "Old soldiers never die."

From advertising:
* ✳ "Where's the beef?"
* ✳ "I love you, man."

From sports:
* ✳ "Say it ain't so, Joe."
* ✳ "Win one for the Gipper."

From exploration:
* ✳ "Dr. Livingston, I presume."
* ✳ "Houston, we have a problem."

From the movies:
* ✳ "Round up the usual suspects."
* ✳ "Frankly my dear, I don't give a damn."
* ✳ "Go ahead, make my day."
* ✳ "Show me the money."

Can You Focus Key Information?

> . . . since brevity is the soul of wit,
> And tediousness the limbs and outward flourishes,

I will be brief.
Your noble son is mad.

Polonius, Hamlet. 2, 2

Polonius's comment about brevity, with wit better defined as wisdom, has often been quoted as a reminder to long-winded speakers to keep it short and to the point. Unfortunately, as one of Shakespeare's most garrulous characters, Polonius was a fine example of "do as I say, not as I do."

DUCHESS   I will be mild and gentle in my speech.

RICHARD   And brief, good mother; for I am in haste.

Richard III. 4, 4

In this era of information overload, it's easy for your information to get lost. As a communicator, your duty often is to call attention to critical problems, significant changes, and impending risks so that decision makers can get the information they need. Present it clearly focused and the receivers can pick it up quickly and sharply. Present it in a roundabout or obscure manner and they may miss it.

Later, in Chapter 15, we'll note the value of the Executive Summary, the concise version of your message. Here's how language can help achieve that:

* Prioritize information.
* Highlight key words.
* Choose the short, snappy phrase versus the convoluted one.
* Make it easier to get with enumeration, bullets versus wordy paragraphs, and sharp segues into a new topic.
* Apply vocal **STRESS**; inflection, pauses . . . ; repetition, I repeat, repetition.

Marlin Fitzwater, as press secretary to President George Bush, found himself under fire from the media during a Panamanian coup incident: "*The Wall Street Journal* had published a lengthy story on the coup, obviously fed by the CIA station chief in Panama. Basically, he was angry that the U.S. government had dropped the ball on his coup attempt, which he had undoubtedly nurtured, so he fed the story of U.S. ineptness to the *Journal*. He was right, of course. *Apparently his reports to CIA headquarters never got transferred to State or Defense, and therefore never fed directly to the president. The CIA's daily written report to the president apparently did mention the contact, but in such an elliptical way that no one caught the significance.*"

Do Your Words Paint Pictures?

> Age cannot wither her, nor custom stale
> Her infinite variety: other women cloy
> The appetites they feed, but she makes hungry
> Where most she satisfies.
>
> Enobarbus, *Antony and Cleopatra.* 2, 2

Language, in the hands of a deft practitioner, can create images as effectively as a paintbrush.

> There is a devil haunts thee in the likeness of an old fat man; a tun of man is thy companion. Why dost thou converse with that trunk of humours, that bolting-hutch of beastliness, that swollen parcel of dropsies, that huge bombard of sack, that stuffed cloak-bag of guts, that roasted Manningtree ox with the pudding in his belly, that reverend vice, that grey iniquity, that father ruffian, that vanity in years? Wherein is he

good, but to taste sack and drink it? wherein neat
and cleanly, but to carve a capon and eat it? wherein
cunning, but in craft? wherein crafty, but in villainy?
wherein villainous, but in all things? wherein worthy,
but in nothing?

Hal, *Henry IV, Part I.* 2, 4

Hal could have described Falstaff in a few words, such as "He's a
bawdy, loudmouthed, fat guy," but he chose to sparkle it up a bit (it
is a drama, and part comedy at that.) Perhaps this fits one of your
colleagues; how much more colorful and richly descriptive these
words are than "You big slob."

Check both your spoken and written language to see if you can
add spice, clarity, and interest to your topic. Here are some suggestions:

* See if there's a better word. Take the word "walked." Would
  one of these work better? Strolled, ambled, drifted,
  wandered, strode, crept, glided, tromped, traversed, hiked,
  moonwalked . . .

* Add descriptive phraseology. "Need to move forward" or
  "Are we ready to fish, or do we continue to cut bait?"

* Try more colorful and often more accurate terminology.
  Instead of "We believe our progressively developing advances
  have rendered the primary competing organization less
  viable," try "They're dead meat."

* Replace wimpy, tentative fudge words with snappier phrases.
  "Very hard" versus "extremely difficult, arduous with a
  capital 'A', formidable beyond our expectations."

* Turn a negative into a positive: "obstacle" versus "challenge"
  or "opportunity."

Using picturesque language may not always be the smartest move, however. Pfeiffers Brewing Co. ran, and quickly pulled, a new ad touting their product as "the beer with the silent P."

Are You an Upbeat or Downbeat Communicator?

> O, to what purpose dost thou hoard thy words,
> That thou return'st no greeting to thy friends?
>
> Gaunt, *Richard II.* 1, 3

How eager are you to engage in dialogue with someone you know to be always in a dour mood, with never a good word for anyone, who always looks for trouble ahead and never the bright side? The person who is more likely to snarl and insult than to help or cheer up? Anybody come to mind? Does that constant negative style add to the team? Do you look forward to working with him or her?

Now does anyone come to mind whom you would describe as a positive communicator? Especially one who makes sense and offers a valuable contribution (note that a cheerful chap can equally be a useless one)? A person whose working relationship is generally one you look forward to rather than avoid?

> All places that the eye of heaven visits
> Are to a wise man ports and happy havens.
>
> Gaunt, *Richard II.* 1, 3

Are you an optimist or a pessimist? Both have a place, and either style can get boring if always on. A test is your response when your teenager with the new driver's license asks to borrow your car. The pessimist says, "No way!" The optimist says, "Why not?" The cynic has done it before and has traded in the good car for a junker.

How 'bout Some Attaboys and Attagirls (for a Change)

> I can no other answer make but thanks,
> And thanks. . . .
>
> Sebastian, *Twelfth Night. 3, 3*

How often do you say "thanks" or "good job" to your colleagues, spouse, or kids? How often do you pass on praise to the dog, or cat, or parakeet? Do you sense an imbalance there?

Something that amazes me often is not receiving a "thank you" from a service representative of a company I'm giving business to. My personal customer service list says that key number 2 in customer service, often omitted, is to say thanks. Key number 1, also violated regularly, is giving a friendly hello to someone when they first walk into the store. Do you recall any instances where these keys were missing, and what your reaction was?

My experience also shows we have an epidemic of failing to thank those who have done something for us. What did you do when someone sent you an interesting article, gave you a fun book, helped you with a good lead, and so on? How about a quick phone call, an e-mail, or—*egads!*—a handwritten note? Go ahead, test it out: send a dozen (50? 100?) colleagues their own individual copy of an important book—say, *Say It Like Shakespeare*—and see how many respond with a thank-you. (Or is their lack of response a possible editorial comment? *Hmm . . .*)

In *The One Minute Manager*, Ken Blanchard offered this small gem of advice: "Try to catch them doing something right." He was asking managers to take a look at how they conduct their relationships with employees, which typically is heavily slanted to fault-finding rather than back-patting.

We also tend to have skewed perceptions about our own practices. How often would you say that you give fellow employees a pat on the back? When *supervisors* were asked that question on a survey, the answer was 82 percent. When their *employees* were asked how often the boss did that, their answer was 13 percent.

When giving positive feedback:

* Apply the time-proven adage, "Praise in public, criticize in private."

* Before going public, consider your method of communicating to ensure other employees won't be ticked off, feeling they worked just as hard for no praise.

* Talk about specific actions or behavior and the benefits achieved. This effort can help the receiver clearly understand the basis and keep their perspective (the fact that they reduced water waste doesn't mean they walk on water). It can also head off the irritation in others who might have concluded the praise is primarily from favoritism or "sucking up."

* Where applicable, involve employees in the selection process. When *they* choose "most valuable," it often goes over better, and may be more accurate, than if *you*, as supervisor, do it. At the Olympics, it's the athletes, not the officials, who decide who carries the flag in the opening and closing ceremonies.

From Peters and Waterman's *In Search of Excellence*; "Above all, when we look at HP, Tupperware, and others, we see a very conscious management effort to do two things: (1) honor with all sorts of positive reinforcement and valuable, completed action by people at the top and more especially way down the line; and (2) seek out a high volume of opportunities for good news swapping." How does your organization stack up?

Language Power on Display

Here are some samples from which you might draw inspiration:

> Cowards die many times before their deaths;
> The valiant never taste of death but once.
> Of all the wonders that I yet have heard,
> It seems to me most strange that men should fear;
> Seeing that death, a necessary end,
> Will come when it will come.
>
> Caesar, Julius Caesar 2, 2

> The quality of mercy is not strain'd,
> It droppeth as the gentle rain from heaven
> Upon the place beneath. . . . It is twice blest;
> It blesseth him that gives, and him that takes.
>
> Portia, The Merchant of Venice. 4, 1

> Now is the winter of our discontent
> Made glorious summer by this sun of York;
> And all the clouds that lour'd upon our house
> In the deep bosom of the ocean buried.
> Now are our brows bound with victorious wreaths;
> Our bruised arms hung up for monuments;
> Our stern alarums changed to merry meetings.
> Our dreadful marches to delightful measures. . . .

Why, I, in this weak piping time of peace,
Have no delight to pass away the time,
Unless to spy my shadow in the sun,
And descant on mine own deformity:
And, therefore, since I cannot prove a lover,
To entertain these fair well-spoken days,
I am determined to prove a villain,
And hate the idle pleasures of these days.

Richard, *Richard III.* 1, 1

Take-Away Ideas

* The words we choose can add power to our communication.

* Language can clarify, edify, and move.

* Check your communication pattern to enhance the positive side.

* Upgrade your language capability, and upgrade your success.

Chapter 6

>⊰≫⊱<

Is Your English Frittered?
Overcoming Language Deficiencies

> They have been at a great feast of languages, and stolen
> the scraps.
>
> Moth, Love's Labour's Lost. 5, 1

Now we'll look at the other side of the language coin, exploring ways
in which the language you use when speaking or writing can interfere
with your communication success. We'll also suggest remedies for
these common language flaws.

Lots of Words Speaking Nothing?

PANDARUS   What says she there?

TROILUS   (*tearing Cressida's letter*)   Words, words, mere
words, no matter from the heart.

Troilus and Cressida. 5, 3

Gratiano speaks a great deal of nothing.

Bassanio, The Merchant of Venice. 1, 1

Can poor language capability really set back your career? People with noticeable language flaws may be eliminating themselves from consideration for positions that require considerable customer contact, such as receptionists, bank tellers, and salespeople. This same deficiency can also pigeonhole someone in a low-level position within an organization.

* During staffing for a proposal with big potential, a talented manager was excluded from the team because of frequent language flubs in meetings and presentations.

* A well-regarded supervisor was a candidate for a vacant managerial position. With reluctance upper management excluded him because his many language errors were not in keeping with the requirements of position.

* In a professional association a faithful member lost out on an open position because it called for many speeches, and the nominating team felt that his language misuse would embarrass the organization.

Can You Be Understood?

> Sir,
> You speak a language that I understand not.
>
> Hermione, *Winter's Tale.* 3, 2

Can you imagine that—a wife having trouble understanding her husband? What's that about men being from Mars and women from Venus?

In the workplace arena, miscommunication occurs all the time. A common lament concerning written communications, such as policy changes and product use directions, from various industries and professions, is that they are hard to decipher. My list of top offenders includes those responsible for legal contracts, computer software manuals, food nutrition labels, and "easy-to-assemble" house projects.

Government and corporations have made many efforts to rewrite complex tomes into more easily understood language. Or have they?

* National Airlines explanation to shareholders, referring to the crash of a Boeing 727 aircraft: "an involuntary conversion of a 727."

* The governmental military specification used for purchases of Worcestershire sauce is a 17-page document.

* From an economist: "We can tell you definitely there will be an easing up at the rate at which business has been easing off. Put another way, there will be a slowing up of the slowdown. By way of explanation, the slowing up of the slowdown is not as good as an upturn in the downturn."

> But those that understood him smiled at one another,
> and shook their heads; but for mine own part, it was
> Greek to me.
>
> Casca (a Roman), *Julius Caesar*. 1, 2

The merger of Chrysler with Daimler-Benz in 1998 resulted in considerable ill will between the two entities, with the U.S. firm apparently receiving shoddy treatment as now the second-class player. "During the early stages of the takeover, some Daimler-Benz officials held meetings with Chrysler staffers and spoke only in German, knowing full well the provincials couldn't understand."

Some people make a specialty of obscuring information, burying it in the fine print. They do that so we layfolk won't suspect it's not all on the up-and-up. Too much clarity can reveal serious flaws.

Trying to decipher ballot propositions, where "yes" may mean "no," frustrates even well-informed voters.

For an upcoming management presentation, I asked the team why a particular chart was so laden with information. "We have a weak case here, so we want to overwhelm them with information and get out without any embarrassing questions." Well, that's one approach.

The long battle for the 2000 presidential race, with the nation's focus on Florida's counts and recounts, was finally shut down by the U.S. Supreme Court. Their 65-page ruling was highly criticized (though not by Republicans) as one of the most convoluted in recent history. With all TV networks on full reporting mode, commentators struggled with the content, handicapped with the lack of a synopsis (standard for such rulings) and with key points scattered—some said buried—in later pages.

> Sir, his definement suffers no perdition in you; though,
> I know, to divide him inventorially would dozy th'
> arithmetic of memory, and yet but yaw neither, in
> respect of his quick sail.
>
> Hamlet, *Hamlet*. 5, 2

Hamlet is speaking intentionally to baffle his receiver, and succeeds admirably. Some of us succeed in baffling our receivers without that intent.

These examples illustrate some of the primary culprits interfering with clarity of language:

* Big words where little ones will do ("obfuscate" vs. "cloud"); ("take corrective action" vs. "fix")

* Terms or acronyms some may not know ("vertical mobilization implementing device" vs. "elevator"; IPT, FICA, ISO . . .)

* Words that are impressive sounding but are made up ("inventorially", "dozy") or vague in meaning ("paradigm"— who understands it?)

* Excessive use of passive versus active tense ("Several tests were conducted" vs. "We ran three tests")

* Metaphors that make sense only to the sender ("yaw" and "sail" in above example)

Are You Bethumping Them with Words?

> Zounds! I was never so bethump'd with words
> Since I first call'd my brother's father dad.
>
> Philip the Bastard, *King John*. 2, 1

Back to brevity being the soul of wit. In many business situations, the minds of the receivers can absorb only so much before they go on overload. I recall a senior executive riffling through a 3-inch-thick report and observing, "Do they really think I will read this?"

Smart trainers, meeting managers, and speakers are careful to stop yapping before their listeners' eyes glaze over.

Bill Clinton has frequently had a problem with his major speeches by continuing on so long the cries of "Hook!" from those present or "zap" from TV remotes occur, most notably at the 1988 Democratic convention when he introduced presidential candidate Michael Dukakis, and again during a State of the Union speech.

Unfortunately, critics often are guilty of the same offenses as those they criticize. Here a chap is lamenting bad English in others:

> I abhor such fanatical phantasimes, such insociable and
> point-devise companions; such rackers of orthogra-
> phy, as to speak dout, fine, when he should say
> doubt; det, when he should pronounce debt,—d, e,
> b, t, not d, e, t: he clepeth a calf, cauf; half, hauf;
> neighbor *vocatur* nebour; neigh abbreviated ne. This
> is abhominable—which he would call abbominable: it
> insinuateth me of insanie: *an-ne intelligis domine?*
>
> Holofernes, *Love's Labour's Lost.* 5, 1

Suggestions to trim excess verbosity:

* Revisit your objective and how best to achieve that. Will an in-depth treatise do that? Or would a concise summary plus dialogue do it better?

* Assess how receivers typically want information. Do they want a full report and lots of detail? Are they a quick study and expect a snapshot and not the whole album?

* Put a page or time limit on your communication. Check with the audience to see if that limitation fits. Then stick to it.

* Organize your material (see tips in Chapter 15). Try ways to condense information such as visual aids.

* For spoken word, keep tuned into your audience. Check before, after, or during the communication to see if they are getting what they want, or if they want something different.

Is Your English Frittered?

Have I lived to stand at the taunt of one that makes
   fritters of English?

Falstaff, *The Merry Wives of Windsor.* 5, 5

"Well, uh, in our polcee we has six key tenants. Me and Jean wrote
it's major parts, hers addressing y'know, nucular weapons reduction,
and mine, being complimentary, covered the second criteria. Causing
big trouble amongst 3rd world nations, we recommend, dude, like,
gittin' the U.N. to back up there principals."

How many, if any, errors in language do you spot in preceding
paragraph?

Here's a fellow frights English out of his wits.

Page, *The Merry Wives of Windsor.* 2, 1

Mistakes in grammar, usage, or fluency will stand out to astute receivers. If you don't believe it, ask George W. Bush, whose many
language miscues during his 2000 presidential campaign kept making
the news. In a speech touting the virtues of the Texas *educational*
testing system, he said, "In 1994, 67 schools were rated exemplerary
by our own tests."

For those in the spotlight who are prone to language goofs, the
next flub always gets a prompt headline and another humorous item
on the late-night talk shows. Does the name Dan Quayle come to
mind? He actually had plenty of company in the political fluffs field,
as these examples from *The 776 Stupidest Things Ever Said* indicate:

*   "Mr. Speaker, this bill is a phony with a capital *F*"
    (congressman during heated debate).

* "That lowdown scoundrel deserves to be kicked to death by a jackass—and I'm just the one to do it" (Texas candidate for Congress, per Massachusetts State Senator John Parker).

* "Why can't the Jews and Arabs just sit down together and settle this like good Christians?" (Congressional debate, also attributed to British statesman Arthur Balfour).

> Here will be an old abusing of God's patience and the king's English.
>
> Mistress Quickly, *The Merry Wives of Windsor*. 1, 4

One of the fastest ways to short-circuit your advancement opportunities is to botch the spoken or written word. Send in a report or put a slide on the screen in a meeting with one or more misspelled words and it's a flag signaling "poor preparation" or "doesn't know any better." Making *Newsweek* was a campaign where students sent large plywood postcards to state lawmakers, one of whom said "I'm going to get a red pen and circle all the mistakes." He flagged out spelling of "Legislture and affordibility." What added to the impact was that the cards came from Iowa State University students.

Not everybody has perfect command of the language, but some of us are way below perfect. If you're one of those, for your career's sake:

* Take a course in language use.

* Get a book on proper and improper usage, and study it.

* Start a personal reference notebook containing your own repeated problem words.

* Join a local Toastmaster's Club to get continued help identifying and correcting verbal goofs.

* Before you go public with your reports and visuals have an astute colleague review them.

> ELBOW   If it please your honour, I am the poor Dukes's constable, and my name is Elbow: I do lean upon justice, sir, and do bring in here before your good honour two notorious benefactors.
>
> ANGELO   Benefactors? Well, what benefactors are they? are they not malefactors?
>
> *Measure for Measure.* 2, 1

Here's a sample of common language errors to look out for. Many of these are demonstrated in the earlier paragraph, but you probably knew that already.

* *The bungled apostrophe.* "Its" or "it's"? Remember, "it's" means "it is." This one is regularly misused in ads by professionals who should know better.

* *Confused word.* "Complementary" (adds to) or "complimentary" (free)? "Tenets" (guidelines) or "tenants" (those who pay rent)? "Principle" (basic guideline) or "principal" (#1)? "Calvary" to the rescue?

* *Singular/plural confusion.* One criteria? Two meeses?

* *Mispronounced words.* How many *u*'s in nuclear? How many a's in athlete.

* *Personal pronoun misuse.* "Me and Jean wrote . . ." "She asked her and I to do it."

* *Noun-verb mismatches.* "The Technicians has . . ."

* *Misplaced modifiers.* "Causing trouble, we recommend . . ."

Activating Brain Before Mouth

Weigh'st thy words before thou givest them breath.

Othello, Othello. 3, 3

Perchance have you ever been guilty of this, making some rash statement or doing some spur-of-the-moment act that later came back to haunt you? If so, welcome to a very large club. "Why did I say that? Why didn't I just shut up? Why didn't I count to ten or even three? Why didn't I pause to reflect first?"

At the close of a large program review meeting, the chairperson went around the group asking if anyone had any open issues. I had been updated earlier on one area needing more attention, which could easily have been addressed in separate session. But I opened my mouth and stated the situation (in part because it showed the prime contractor in a somewhat bad light). The meeting erupted, and while I did embarrass the prime, it was clearly a totally unnecessary and stupid comment. Why do I still remember that, from a meeting 30 years ago?

> Such stuff as madmen
> Tongue, and brain not.

Posthumus, Cymbeline. 5, 4

These gaffes stand out in the political realm because they're on public display. In the 1976 presidential debate with Jimmy Carter, President Gerald Ford stated that Poland was not under the dominance of the Soviet Union. This became the major topic of the debate and was ranked the biggest miscue of the campaign, which Gerald Ford lost.

In 1974 the Ford administration was beset with inflation and unemployment creating major economic problems. Commenting on the effects of those problems, Alan Greenspan, head of the President's Council of Economic Advisors, said Wall Street brokers were "hurt the most" by inflation, a remark that was greeted with guffaws from the laboring classes. Not one of the more well-thought-out remarks from the current economic czar, whose every word is now greeted with intense interest.

Senate Armed Services Committee Chairman John Warner pulled a dandy during hearings on military readiness. It happened to be at the peak of the 2000 presidential campaign, where that was a key issue. General Henry Shelton, chairman of the Joint Chiefs of Staff, was using a chart illustrating drops in weapons purchases, which led Warner, a Republican, to declare this showed that the big cut started "when the change of administration occurred in 1990."

Naturally, Senator Carl Levin, a Democrat, couldn't pass up such an opportunity, noting that President Clinton did not take office until 1993; thus the big drop occurred during the previous, (President Bush's) term. The general agreed with Levin: "Oh, yes sir. I think the chart clearly shows that."

> Oh God, that men should put an enemy in their
> mouths to steal away their brains.
>
> Cassio, *Othello*. 2, 3

Here are a few other examples of mouth going without brain adequately in charge.

* Los Angeles Chief of Police Daryl Gates, explaining why the choke hold seemed to be killing more blacks than others: ". . . in some blacks when the hold is applied, the veins or arteries do not open up like . . . in normal people." Guess how well this went over.

* Religious broadcaster and past presidential candidate Pat Robertson, referred to Scotland as a "dark land" because it

tolerates homosexuals. The Bank of Scotland then canceled a planned joint business venture.

* Pro basketball star Shawn Kemp in an interview said his favorite sneakers as a kid were Nikes. His sponsor, Reebok, terminated his lucrative endorsement contract.

Is there a remedy? How about before speaking on a topic of some concern and involving some risk, pause a few seconds and review quickly in your mind what you are about to say. Or, if you have spouted off and out came clearly the wrong statement, try to rectify it immediately. Make it a clarification, not an apology.

Holding Tongue When We Need to Hear You?

> Why do we hold our tongues,
> That most may claim to this argument for ours?
> [i.e., when we are most concerned about the issue]
>
> Malcolm, *Macbeth*. 2, 3

When you have important information, and you know people are making decisions based on faulty information, your failing to speak up may let a bad course of action proceed.

Early in the space program, a colleague discovered a flaw in the guidance system just before a space booster was to lift off with an expensive satellite. In a large meeting surrounded by high-level managers, he took the risk of pointing out this mistake. Immediately challenged, he calmly presented his findings. They investigated and stopped the launch. He received public praise for this action. This may be risky if you're low on the totem pole or the boss is a poor receiver, especially of news that might not match his own mindset.

Seymour Hersh in *The Price of Power* described the tense situation during the Vietnam War in 1969 when the United States started bombing in Cambodia. At issue was how much to reveal to Congress and the public. Included in the debate were Secretary of Defense Melvin Laird and Secretary of State William Rogers, who believed public disclosure was important, and Henry Kissinger, National Security Advisor, who opposed it. Nixon was already inclined toward Kissinger's position of secrecy. "Laird and Rogers made the error of telling the President (Nixon) what they really thought. Kissinger knew better." The bombing stayed secret, until later, when all hell broke loose.

During the time when Senator Joe McCarthy was hurling the label of Communist at many people, President Dwight Eisenhower remained silent, even when McCarthy went after the State Department, the Army, or Ike's World War II colleague Gen. George Marshall. Later, in his diary Ike wrote, "At times, one feels like hiding his head in shame."

Are You a Name Caller?

Either thou art most ignorant by age,
Or thou wert born a fool.

Leontes, *The Winter's Tale.* 2, 1

How helpful are the words you use when communicating with colleagues, friends, or family? One of the most damaging techniques is labeling, such as during disputes or when giving feedback to others. Labeling seems to be more prevalent in many forms of communication, as demonstrated every day by talk radio shows dealing with controversial issues. It's much easier to call those who disagree with you blithering idiots than to discuss the issue or give them a chance to state their case.

How useful or effective would the following communication from a supervisor to a subordinate be? "You keep coming in late. You're a lazy bum, have a poor attitude, and are an undependable goof-off." Can you see the recipient's hostility surface instantly? What are the chances of the employee changing his or her behavior?

Suppose the supervisor said instead, "We need to discuss your history of showing up late. Over the past two weeks you've shown up late six out of ten days, and over two hours late on three of these. This causes problems with our productivity as others are held up waiting on your output. What do you suggest we do about this?"

In the first example, the supervisor is *name calling*. In the second, the supervisor is focusing *on specific behavior and its effects*. Big difference.

Are You Using the Blunt-Instrument Approach?

> Rude am I in my speech,
> And little blest with the soft phrase of peace.
>
> Othello, *Othello.* 1, 3

In some situations a firm, concise, to-the-point statement is appropriate. I doubt that a SWAT squad needs much more than "Go! Go! Go!"

In other situations some people use the blunt-instrument style when a more tactful, sensitive approach would achieve better results. This applies especially to sending bad news or advising colleagues of changes that affect them.

President Lincoln responded to a complaint from Secretary of War Stanton about a general who had hurled some accusation his way, with the suggestion "Prick him hard!" Stanton readily agreed and wrote out a strongly worded letter. He showed it to Lincoln, who said it was first-rate. When Stanton started to mail it, Lincoln interrupted him: "You don't want to sent that letter. Put it in the stove. That's what I do when I've written a letter when I'm angry. Now burn it and write another letter."

Jacob Braude, in *Braude's Treasury of Wit and Humor*, clarifies the difference:

> The captain approached the sergeant with a bit of bad news. "Sergeant," he said, "we just got notice that Smith's grandmother died. You'd better go break the news to him."
>
> The sergeant walked into the barracks, paused at the doorway, and shouted, "Hey, Smith, your grandmother died."
>
> The captain was horrified. "Sergeant, that's no way to tell a man his grandmother has died. Look how you've shocked him. You have to use tact in a situation like this. I think we'd better send you to Tact and Diplomacy School."
>
> So the sergeant spent a year studying at the Tact and Diplomacy School. On the day he returned, the captain approached him.
>
> "Well, sergeant, how did you do in school?"
>
> "Fine," replied the sergeant. "I've really learned how to be tactful."
>
> "That's good, because we've just gotten notice that Lopez's grandmother died. Go in and tell him."
>
> The sergeant entered the barracks, paused at the doorway and called his men to attention. When they were all lined up he stepped before them and ordered, "All those with living grandmothers, step forward. Not so fast, Lopez."

Heavy-Handed at Addressing Problems?

You peasant swain! You whoreson malt-horse drudge!
Did I not bid thee meet me in the park,
And bring along these rascal knaves with thee?

Petruchio, *The Taming of the Shrew.* 4, 1

Does this resemble your mode of communicating with your team, your underlings? If not you, I'll bet you've seen other managers operate this way. Aren't they fun to work for or around?

> LAERTES   The devil take thy soul!
>
> HAMLET   Thou prayest not well.
> I prithee, take thy fingers from my throat.
>
> *Hamlet.* 5, 1

Sounds like some conflict resolution training might be a good investment for this team. Basketball fans will recognize this as the Latrell Sprewell approach to addressing issues with management: To heck with the open door, go for the open throat.

> Could I come near your beauty with my nails,
> I'd set my ten commandments in your face.
>
> Duchess of Gloucester, *Henry VI, Part 2.* 1, 3

If this represents your approach to resolving disputes, your needs may be far beyond the modest ideas presented here. Might I suggest a quick visit to a therapist before your communication prowess really gets you into trouble.

> By this hand, I will supplant some of your teeth.
>
> Stephano, *The Tempest.* 3, 2

Likewise, we've got some real work to do here. Or is this dialogue from a World Wrestling Federation script? Yes? Then it's perfectly fine.

Checking my morning newspaper sports page, I noted three stories of athletic figures once more in big trouble because of communication miscues: John Rocker, Tonya Harding, and Bobby Knight.

I was looking for a piece on Mike Tyson to make a quartet of terrific communicators.

Are You Foul-Mouthed?

> Hang him, swaggering rascal! Let him no come hither:
> it is the foul-mouthedst rogue in England.
>
> Doll Tearsheet, *Henry IV, Part 2. 2, 4*

A simple way to limit your career options in today's business environment is to use foul language or other troublesome phraseology in the wrong place or with the wrong group. It's OK to tell raunchy jokes with your pals in the saloon; don't try it in the meeting at work. As heard on the Watergate tapes, Richard Nixon was a great practitioner of private profanity, though it rarely appeared in public communication. Lyndon Johnson also was prone to pithy language in personal communication, but rarely in public.

Putdowns (intended or inadvertent), sexist references, and ethnic quips can lead to costly career and legal problems. For example,

* Mr. Sensitivity, James Watt, President Reagan's Secretary of the Interior, referring to staff in his agency, said, "We have every mixture you can have. I have a black, I had a woman, two Jews and a cripple."

* Coach Bobby Knight, in an interview, said, "If rape is inevitable, you might as well enjoy it." He claimed it was taken out of context.

* Dr. Laura (Schlesinger) referred to gays as "biological errors" and "deviant." The pickets are regular visitors at her appearances.

* A male broker sent a package to a female colleague. In it were a sex toy, lubricating cream, and an obscene poem. When management failed to act, an embarrassing lawsuit resulted.

In the age of e-mail, it's easy to launch a diatribe against a colleague that proves later to be unwise, especially if that message gets copied to twenty-five other people. Then you may be perceived not as someone with a lament but as an insensitive hothead, racist, or sexist. Before you send a negative missive, print it out, take another look at it, and perhaps ask a colleague to review it.

If you're a speaker or a trainer, it's a good idea to rehearse your material in front of others, to get their feedback before you go public with it. You can also ask participants to fill out a feedback sheet, as they may feel safer telling you something negative anonymously. Take those comments seriously.

Take-Away Ideas

* Poor language can be a serious detriment to your success and advancement.

* Many people are unaware of their language mistakes, either spoken or written.

* Get feedback to identify your own verbal flaws, and start a campaign to fix, correct, and even rectify them.

* Speak up when your input is needed.

* Think before sending messages that might offend others and truly set back your career.

Chapter 7

Suit the Action to the Word:
Body Language That Works for You

I do not much dislike the matter, but
The manner of his speech.

Octavius Caesar, Antony and Cleopatra. 2, 2

Fie, fie upon her!
There's language in her eye, her cheek, her lip,
Nay, her foot speaks; her wanton spirits look out
At every join and motive of her body.

Ulysses, Troilus and Cressida. 4, 5

What makes up nonverbal communication? From Ulysses' comment, and ample research, many things. Eye contact, facial expression, physical appearance, tone of voice, body movement, wardrobe—all of these have a big effect on the impressions intended and received.

They seemed almost, with staring on one another, to
    tear the cases of their eyes; there was speech in their
    dumbness, language in their very gesture; they
    looked as they had heard of a world ransomed, or

one destroyed; a notable passion of wonder appeared
in them.

First Gentleman, *Winter's Tale.* 5, 2

Body Language Speaks Volumes

Good morrow, Benedick. Why, what's the matter,
That you have such a February face,
So full of frost, of storm, and cloudiness?

Don Pedro, *Much Ado About Nothing.* 5, 4

As receivers, we start assessing the nature of the communication before a word is spoken. Then as communication continues, we con-
tinuously and subconsciously color our interpretations based on our
nonverbal perceptions. These perceptions have been developed
throughout our lives; some are common to groups of people with
the same experiences and background, while others are personal,
acquired from our own life experiences.

By his face straight shall you know his heart.

Hastings, *Richard III.* 3, 4

Press Secretary Marlin Fitzwater, in *Call the Briefing*, described the
preparation for a key press conference by President George Bush
when the Berlin Wall came down in 1989. This was a ticklish topic,
an exciting event but requiring care not to gloat:

I gave him some talking points on the logistics of the wall coming
down: when, at what location, reaction from some world leaders,
etc. He read them and started walking toward the Oval (office).
He opened the door and all the lights came on. He walked to
his desk, sat down, and said a few words about the historic
moment.

But from the beginning, he seemed uninspired. As he continued, the president did the one thing that made every Bush staffer start to sweat. He started sliding down in his chair. It was the absolutely ironclad signal that he didn't like what he was doing, didn't want to be there, and was probably going to show it.

Soon he was talking in a monotone, his head bowed and hands folded across his chest. . . . George Bush just could never hide his feelings. If he was happy or excited, his arms would flail and his eyes would dance around a smile that twisted all over his face. But if he was reluctant, or distracted, the lines in his face would deepen and his eyes would glaze over in seconds. He was now in full glaze.

We Place High Reliance on Nonverbal Information

In thy face, I see
The map of honor, truth, and loyalty.

Henry VI, *Henry VI, Part 2. 3, 1*

A lot of pressure has been put on the International Olympic Committee regarding bribery for votes in host city selection. Within the United States a special three-member committee was formed to determine if the IOC was truly going to make changes to eliminate the bribery. Ken Duberstein, a committee member, told of a critical meeting where the IOC head attempted to convince them they were serious. "We all had serious doubts," he said. "As Samaranch spoke we were looking for facial twitches, for aversion of eyes." The nonverbal factor was key to their believing that Samaranch and the IOC were sincere.

How much do we credit the words as spoken, and how much the nonverbal channels? The answer follows.

HAMLET   What make you at Elsinore?

ROSENCRANTZ   To visit you, my lord; no other occasion.

HAMLET   . . . Were you not sent for? Is it your own
inclining? Is it a free visitation? Come, come, deal justly
with me. Come, come; nay, speak.

GUILDENSTERN   What should we say, my lord?

HAMLET   Why anything—but to the purpose. You were
sent for; and there is a kind of confession in your looks,
which your modesties have not craft enough to colour. I
know the good king and queen have sent for you.

Hamlet. 2, 2

Hamlet is convinced the two visitors are lying, almost before they've said anything. Border patrol officers, from questioning thousands of people, have developed their lie detector faculties to a keen edge. Combine this with our own typically amateurish ability to lie, and you can see why they have a good idea when we're covering up about the six quarts of tequila hidden in the car's trunk, leading to those dreaded words, "Pull over there; let's take a look."

Back to the earlier question: how much do we credit the spoken versus nonspoken. Many studies have been done testing this proposition, with generally consistent results. The most-reported one cites Albert Mehrabian's research that, under certain conditions, only 7 percent of our interpretation comes from the spoken words; the other 93 percent we pick up from nonverbal factors. The primary application of these findings is that when we perceive a mismatch between the spoken and nonspoken message, we overwhelmingly apply the nonspoken interpretation.

> How tartly that gentleman looks! I never can see him
> but I am heart-burned an hour after.
>
> Beatrice, *Much Ado About Nothing.* 2, 1

During the 2000 presidential campaign, a constant key issue (it seemed) was the candidates' body language: George W. Bush's smirk and Al Gore's "look." I watched Bush closely during his acceptance speech at the Republican National Convention and can report not one smirk (though it appeared several times that he was on the verge of one but stifled it). Then in the first presidential debate, the big story was less what Al Gore said but more his nonverbal reactions to what his opponent said. Did Gore's rolling eyes, loud sighs, and disgusted expressions play a part in his losing the election? He cut those out during debates 2 and 3.

> Tell me where is fancy bred,
> Or in the heart, or in the head?
> How begot, how nourished?
> Reply, reply.
> It is engendered in the eyes.
>
> Song, *The Merchant of Venice.* 3, 2

In Western culture, we have strong reactions to eye contact. When others tell us something, we are likely to believe it if they look us in the eye, and we are wary if they don't. This can present problems in business, where employees bring different cultural backgrounds.

Tiger Woods speaks often to young aspiring golfers. "There were quite a few who, when they shook my hand, wouldn't look me in the eye. I said 'If you want to be a man, look 'em square in the eye.' " In some cultures, this might well be bad, not good, advice.

Be a Congruent Communicator

This above all: to thine own self be true,
And it must follow, as the night the day,
Thou canst not then be false to any man.

Polonius, *Hamlet*. 1, 3

Know you have a good story, be certain that your proposal is an honest one, believe it's good for you and the audience, and communicate that with sincerity and appropriate passion.

His words come from his mouth, ours from our breast.

Duchess of York, *King Richard II*. 5, 3

I was coaching a program manager for a major proposal. Before the rehearsal he was running the team meeting, giving orders, and setting action items, all in a forceful, emphatic manner. We then shifted to rehearsal, and he started his presentation in a wooden, mechanical style, not at all resembling the real person we'd just seen running the meeting. He went into some sort of speaker's zone. I showed him the video of the two selves he'd displayed, and he was taken aback. He agreed that he'd apparently stepped into the wrong phone booth, and instead of Superman, out came Superwimp. In the next rehearsal the real leader showed up. The lesson is, let the real you show up.

For Harry, now I do not speak to thee in drink but in
tears; not in pleasure but in passion; not in words
only, but in woes also.

Falstaff, *Henry IV, Part 1*. 2, 4

If you strive for truly open communication, let your entire body communicate (ignoring the fact that Falstaff is faking it). Speak from the heart, not just from the throat. A caveat here: Do not take this too far if you're at the poker table. When you have four aces and let it all hang out, don't be surprised when the winnings are puny.

Suit the Action to the Word

> Nor do not saw the air too much with your hand . . .
> Suit the action to the word, the word to the action.
>
> Hamlet (to the Players), *Hamlet*. 3, 2

An important attribute for an effective communicator, is to be natural and congruent, and maintain a match between body and spoken language. Senders often have difficulty doing this. The speaker says, "We strongly support your approach and are eager to get going on this project" with quavering voice, a wooden stance, and hands gesturing nervously. Will the receivers of these mixed messages believe the words or the actions?

For most of us, the body usually finds it hard to deceive. In helping an executive prepare for a legal hearing, we posed a series of questions and observed the responses, plus we videotaped them. On some sensitive areas, such as where he felt some injustice, his body language didn't match his spoken words. We felt that the jury would pick up on this and suspect some fudging was at work. This helped him to clarify his true feelings and come across honestly (which in this case the advisors felt was a sound course).

> Out, damned spot! out, I say! . . . What, will these
> hands ne'er be clean?
>
> Lady Macbeth, *Macbeth*. 5, 1

A common question I get from speakers is "What do I do with my hands?" And a common problem is that speakers do not make good use of their hands. Some will "saw the air" excessively, which can be entertaining and dangerous if the hand holds a pointer. Others go into the gripping (perhaps praying), twisting (especially of pens or pointers), or flailing mode. Remember the testimony of Humphrey Bogart as Captain Queeg in *Mutiny on the Bounty*. The camera kept zeroing in on his gripping hands, with the inference that he was lying.

Others don't let their hands enter into the communication process at all. Their hands hang and grip in front (the well-known fig leaf position), hang at their sides (simulating Frankenstein's monster), flicker lightly (perhaps to drive gnats away), or apply a two-handed death grip to the lectern.

Check your overall message when you communicate with hands gripping. Your body looks tight, your shoulders slump, you appear defensive, and the audience's attention goes directly to those frozen hands. Ungrip those hands and let them into the action. Then we'll see a more forceful, natural communicator, and we probably won't even notice whether the hands are involved or not.

Breathing Life into a Stone

> I have seen a medicine
> That's able to breathe life into a stone,
> Quicken a rock, and make you dance canary
> With spritely fire and motion.
>
> Lafeu, *All's Well That Ends Well*. 2, 1

This medicine I could put to good use. When placed in certain situations, such as being asked to "say a few words," many people go into a wooden communication mode. They stop smiling, squelch their physical animation, look at the wall or their notes, barely move their lips, and speak in monotone. This might be the same person who a few minutes before, at the coffee table, was vigorously telling you about how the kid hit the winning run last night at Little League.

Many pundits have rated Vice President Al Gore's speaking style as wooden. He poked fun at himself about that impression at the 1996 Democratic Convention by showing his version of the macarana (a lively dance, in case you missed that) by standing immobile. During the 2000 presidential campaign the Gore team worked hard to liven up the body language. Commentator Mary McGrory described the reaction at the national convention: "Al Gore's acceptance speech was good. It wasn't great—no poetry or music—but nobody thought he could 'touch men's hearts with glory.' It had the homely virtue of sincerity. Democrats who had endured the long months of his endless reinventions said, in relief and gratitude as they streamed out of the Staples Center with confetti in their hair, 'It was him.' "

Suit Your Action to the Culture

> Those that are good manners at the court are as
>   ridiculous in the country as the behaviour of the
>   country is most mockable at the court. You told me
>   you salute not at the court, but you kiss your hands:
>   that courtesy would be uncleanly, if courtiers were
>   shepherds.
>
> Corin, *As You Like It.* 3, 2

It's hard enough to be able to read each other's body language when you work in the same building with people who look and respond much as you do. With today's multinational corporations and interlocking relationships, you may find yourself in meetings with people from different geographic and cultural backgrounds. The opportunities for protocol slip-ups, misunderstandings, and inadvertent behavioral goofs are ample. This applies for American to Chinese, or Chinese to Italian.

How well prepared are you or your colleagues when called upon to operate in, or when hosting visitors from, one or more other countries? Here's an indicator from *The World Competitiveness Report*, 1995. They asked over 3000 executives from around the world to rate countries on how well developed "intercultural understanding" is in their business communities. Switzerland, Singapore, Netherlands, Hong Kong, and Malaysia were the top five. The United States was way down at #35, just ahead of Portugal and Hungary, with the United Kingdom even below that.

If you are about to engage with people in a different culture, be aware that trouble may lie ahead. Then get some advice from others who have operated in that environment. Have them review your reports, presentations, and meeting plans before engagement. Here are some typical trouble spots, from an American business perspective:

* *Protocol.* With non-Americans, the standard for introductions may be more formalized.

* *Action focus.* The U.S. style of "no nonsense, let's get to it, cut to the chase, let's close" can be totally opposite to others.

* *Interpreting body language.* If you're used to interacting one on one or in groups with people much like yourself, meeting with someone from another culture may lead to misunderstandings.

* *Contact.* Sidney Jourard, in *Disclosing Man to Himself*, noted how touch can be easily misconstrued. He watched people interacting in coffee shops and counted how many times they touched each other in one hour. The findings were: San Juan, 180; Paris, 110; London, 0; Gainesville, Florida, 2.

Can you see potential trouble when that Puerto Rican meets the Londoner?

* *Pressure.* An American's schedule may involve a 30-minute quick-grab lunch and 15-hour day—to hell with the family. Another person, when working on a team basis, may not want to operate in that style. Both might get irritated.

* *Niceties.* In the United States refreshments might consist of coffee with Styrofoam cups, sweet rolls, and plastic spoons. To others that may seem crude.

* *Pushing for decision.* In the United States one person may be able to make a commitment; elsewhere it may require several phases and groups.

John Norton heads the International Resource Center, a firm consulting with business in many countries. He notes some common nonverbal styles that, to the rest of the world, make Americans seem strange (and may cause problems for you):

* *Informality.* Americans try to be your "buddy" before they even know you. They use your first name without regard to your status or how well they know you.

* *Overconfidence.* The standard positive "can-do" attitude is pushy, boisterous, and very direct.

* *Peculiar sense of humor.* The custom of "kidding" or "poking fun" (even saying insulting things and then laughing) is particularly offensive.

* *Confrontational style.* Americans tend to believe truth can best be reached through arguing about it, not through harmony.

Speaking of Manners

> When didst thou see me heave up my leg, and make
> water against a gentlewoman's farthingale? Didst thou
> ever see me do such a trick?
>
> Launce, *The Two Gentlemen of Verona.* 4, 4

You don't have to be in a "foreign" environment to have ways of interacting that might interfere with the purpose of your communication. Think about your own experiences. What did someone do that led you to feel uncomfortable, embarrassed, irritated, and with a strong desire to end this encounter quickly? Or who comes to mind as someone to emulate, because their style is positive, considerate, and attractive?

How would you rather be seen, as a slob to avoid or as a role model? Failure to pay attention to the little things can definitely impede your getting hired, selected for a key position, making a sale, or getting that date (yes, all this applies to relationships outside the workplace as well).

Consultant Barbara Pachter has conducted seminars in business etiquette for over ten years. She tells of a business deal that went sour because of poor social graces. The corporate executive had taken the potential customer to dinner in an upscale restaurant. It ended up with the customer backing out of a potential $30 million deal. Why did that happen? Said Pachter, "He licked his knife clean."

> There's no more faith in thee than in a stewed prune.
>
> Falstaff, *Henry IV, Part 1.* 3, 3

Here are some other factors, mostly in the common sense category:

* *Personal grooming and hygiene.* We have a high tolerance for individuality, but it's still hard to tell someone their deodorant isn't working.

* *Social manners.* We don't expect others to maintain stiff rigidity to someone's rules, but when they gobble the pizza, shout crude jokes across the cubicle, make embarrassing personal comments, blow smoke in your direction, and send offensive e-mails—do we need this? Did I mention cell phones or sitting in the boss's chair?

* *Consideration for others.* Greet others with courtesy, and then give them your attention instead of flitting in and out for any interruption. Reserve criticism for private, not public, discussion.

* *Respect.* Don't put others down because of their position, race, or sex. Don't toss your lunch trash into the bushes (or beer cans on the beach), and pick up after your dog.

* *Honesty, fair play, genuineness.* Be ethical in carrying out the business, and straight in the relationship.

* *Dependability.* Meet commitments to others and the team.

* *Control.* Don't slam the phone down on someone or unload via e-mail, copied to the entire floor.

* *Acknowledgment.* Say thanks or send a note when someone has done something good for the team or you personally.

We all know at least one of these: witty (or is that sarcastic?), snappy (or is that cutting?), outgoing (or is that obnoxious?), jolly (or is that pushy?), a back-slapper (or is that an abuser?). This is the person possessed of some good attributes who goes over the line with them. We probably display some of these . . . OK, I plead guilty, sometimes. Do we know when we've crossed over the line and have become a real pain in the butt and a person to be avoided?

A caution: It's easy to get overly judgmental about the personal behavior of others. An article on this topic noted one executive who rejected a candidate because when the two went to lunch, the candidate picked up the wrong fork. In the executive's zeal for the "correct" social graces, he may have just rejected another Albert Einstein (needed a haircut) or Apple Computer founder Steve Wozniak (too scruffy).

If you've not had much exposure to this sort of thing, invest in a good book on business etiquette, read the advice columns, ask others you admire for advice, and do a periodic self-check.

> Three times was his nose discharged against me; he
> stands there like a mortar-piece, to blow us.
>
> Man, *Henry VIII*. 5, 4

Perhaps you're saying I'm pushing this behavior thing to absurdity. Nose-blowing on another person? Well, pro football fans might recall an incident where a San Diego Chargers quarterback unloaded on a reporter who'd apparently said less-than-favorable things about his performance.

From Ken Lloyd's "Workplace Q&A" column: "We have a visitor to our office once a week . . . The problem is that he has terrible odor, dirty clothing, and filthy hands." The visitor is a physician.

Or Do You Want to Smile and Be a Villain?

> One may smile and smile, and be a villain.
>
> Hamlet, *Hamlet*. 1, 5

On the other hand, through constant practice some professionals have honed the art of successful lying to a fine art. Maybe you have heard some of these lines:

* "The check is in the mail."
* "And the best part, you don't have to pay anything."
* "Trust me. You can't lose on this investment."
* "Sorry, all those good tables have been reserved" (a Las Vegas classic).

In my poker-playing days, I was perceived to be a cautious bettor. The one time I drew four aces, I started grinning widely. I didn't want to do that, but my mouth and eyes weren't following my orders to go into poker-face position. When I placed a large bet, the other players knew I had a tough hand and they all dropped, leaving me with meager winnings—for four aces! Being not a total dummy, I later tried a bluff with a marginal hand, hoping everybody would drop. I grinned as before, but they spotted a liar immediately. They stayed; I lost.

> Seldom he smiles, and smiles in such a sort as if he mock'd himself.
>
> Caesar, *Julius Caesar*. 1, 2

An honest smile is generally well received by others. Magic Johnson won many fans over because of his broad smile, combined with talent and flair. Yet smiling doesn't come easily to everybody. A favorite skit on *Saturday Night Live* was the actor playing Senator Bob Dole having a hard time smiling. Dole's advisors tried to get him to smile more, but it usually came across forced. Columnist Mike Royko said,

"It's Dole's misfortune that when he does smile, he looks as if he's just evicted a widow."

> Your face, my thane, is as a book where men
> May read strange matters. To beguile the time,
> Look like the time; bear welcome in your eye,
> Your hand, your tongue. Look like the innocent flower,
> But be the serpent under't.
>
> Lady Macbeth, *Macbeth*. 1, 5

Thus, if your occupation is one that prizes the ability to tailor your verbal/nonverbal package at will, it may behoove you to hone this talent. While certainly useful in poker, would this skill be useful in negotiation, sales of a shaky nature, or politics?

> Why, I can smile, and murder whiles I smile,
> And cry "Content!" to that which grieves my heart,
> And wet my cheeks with artificial tears,
> And frame my face to all occasions.
>
> Gloucester (later Richard III), *Henry VI, Part 3. 3*, 2

Sometimes fibbing a bit is actually a wise course of action: "No, of course that outfit doesn't make you look too fat."

Take-Away Ideas

* Body language is a major part of communication.
* Receivers get confused when body language and spoken word don't match.

* Let your body communicate naturally for congruent communication.

* Body language of both senders and receivers can aid or hamper communication.

* Be aware of the impact of your behavior on customers and colleagues.

Chapter 8

> ---✦✦✦---

Let the Apparel Proclaim the Man (and Woman): Appearance As a Positive Factor

> Costly thy habit as thy purse can buy,
> But not express'd in fancy; rich, not gaudy:
> For the apparel oft proclaims the man.
>
> Polonius, *Hamlet*. 1, 3

How important is appearance to achieving a positive impression with audiences? Polonius's comment is one of Shakespeare's most quoted. So let's examine how to have appearance help you.

Appearance: The First Impression

> See where she comes, apparell'd like the spring
>
> Pericles (talking of the king's daughter), *Pericles*. 1, 1

Dress and grooming can quickly establish credibility or disdain. You'll find many books dealing solely with business dress, with studies showing positive and negative results from wearing blue versus brown, long versus shoulder length hair, designer versus casual shoes, and so on. In recent years a more casual wardrobe has replaced the conservative looks of a decade ago. Business dress articles used to deal with the appropriateness of pastel versus white shirts, the acceptability of brown and pantsuits for women. Now the typical article covers casual versus too casual.

In deciding what wardrobe to wear for your upcoming event, several factors warrant consideration. Knowing what is appropriate should be high on the list. Does the situation call for a conservative business look, such as a major presentation or meeting with the board of directors? Even in the high-tech world of casual everyday, what does that pioneer of casual, Bill Gates, wear when communicating across the table with Congress? Good old suit and tie—Mr. Conservative.

Perhaps that reliable dark blue suit might be too conservative for some situations. I was asked to coach a CEO for an upcoming all-hands meeting. He was wearing a blazer, unbuttoned, which he chose intentionally, as he wanted to remove some of the standard barriers that can divide people in organizations. A top financial advisor was invited to speak to a high school economics class; he decided that his typical business suit would create barriers with the class, so he showed up in more casual dress, and achieved a good interaction.

During the 2000 presidential race, much attention was paid to the wardrobe transformation of Vice President Al Gore, the Democratic candidate. To gain better rapport with the electorate, he replaced the standard business suit with an open-shirt, earth-toned wardrobe. That change was given some credit for showing a more personal candidate. Later, when George W. Bush was asked to rebut the statement that he was an "empty suit," he said, "Well, at least not an earth-tone suit."

Appearance Affects Attitude

Methinks I play as I have seen them do
In Whitsun pastorals: sure this robe of mine
Does change my disposition.

Perdita, The Winter's Tale. 4, 4

In one of my training seminars a woman did well at making a presentation, except her appearance, slightly post-hippie, was not helping her much. With some friendly feedback and her own video check, she decided to make some changes. She called me three months later with a report: "As a result of the seminar, I modified my wardrobe to something more appropriate for the organization. I changed my hairstyle and got in better shape. Several managers have commented that I seem to be taking my job more seriously."

In preparing teams for major presentations, a full dress rehearsal can be helpful. Having speakers and audience members dress as they would for the actual event adds more realism to the practice session (and also identifies some weird appearance items, correctable before the real thing).

In many situations—seeking promotion or a new job, testifying in court, going before an academic panel—knowing that your wardrobe is making a positive statement adds to your assurance (and ups the chances of success). In getting people ready for such situations, we dry-run the upcoming interview and then review the videotape to let them see the impact—plus or minus—their appearance and manner might have.

A charitable women's organization called Dressing for Success is helping homeless and poor women upgrade their appearances to improve their chances of landing jobs. The changes are dramatic—the entire attitude is transformed, and they are getting jobs.

But Don't Overestimate Appearance

He came ever in the rearward of the fashion.

Falstaff, Henry IV, Part 2. 3, 2

A scruffy-looking fellow wandered into a bank and said he wanted to transact business. The teller looked at him with disdain and refused to deal with him, assuming he was another homeless street person. He turned out to be a millionaire with a very large account at this bank—past tense, as he withdrew all his money due to the shabby treatment he'd been given.

O that I were a fool!
I am ambitious for a motley coat.

Jaques, As You Like It. 2, 7

One of the members of a proposal team had a different view of appropriate business dress from the other team members; his unusual choice of business wardrobe created a few snickers around the conference room. When he spoke his piece, the snickers ceased as it became obvious he was clearly knowledgeable about a primary area of concern. He could have been wearing bib overalls and it would not have mattered, as he totally won over his audience. (In Jaques' world, the fools—the ones with the motley coats—could speak the truth without fear of consequences.)

There can be no kernel in this light nut; the soul of
this man is his clothes. Trust him not in matter of
heavy consequence.

Lafeu, All's Well That Ends Well. 2, 5

Years back my company invited potential bidders to come in and present their credentials for a planned subcontract. The primary presenter was the finest-looking fellow on the team and an excellent speaker. When the dialogue phase started, it became clear that his knowledge was thin, so several reviewers concluded he must not be part of the technical organization—the workers—but was (gasp!) from sales. There was not much behind the fine look and talk. That hurt the team's chances.

Cover the Full Package

> His garments are rich, but he wears them not
> handsomely.
>
> Shepherd, The Winter's Tale. 4, 4

Beyond the appropriate wardrobe, consider other factors that might work for or against you. If your outfit is not well matched, it can call attention to itself, negatively.

> Get your apparel together, good strings to your beard,
> new ribbons to your pumps; meet presently at the
> palace; every man look o'er his part. . . . Let Thisby
> have clean linen; and let him not that plays the lion
> pare his nails, for they shall hang out for the lion's
> claws.
>
> Bottom, A Midsummer Night's Dream. 4, 2

Does it catch your eye if the fellow you're communicating with is wearing a dark suit with pants two inches above a pair of white socks? Garish tie, hanging loose? Wrinkled shirt? Scruffy jogging shoes? Now those beard strings—haven't those come back in fashion?

You're interviewing a woman for a job opening. You check the three-inch fingernails, the jangling earrings, the nose ring, the tattoo on the neck. "You say you want a customer contact position?"

With his doublet all unbraced:
No hat upon his head; his stockings fouled,
Ungartered and down-gyved to his ankle;
Pale as his shirt; his knees knocking each other;
And with a look so piteous in purport
As if it had been loosed out of hell
To speak of horrors.

Ophelia (describing Hamlet as having gone mad), *Hamlet*. 2, 1

For a crash course on appearance distractors, check Scott Adams's daily cartoon *Dilbert*. Dilbert himself always wears his tie curled up at half-mast; the techies wear pocket protectors with multiple pencils; the irritating women have funny hairdos; the boss has pointy hair; marketing people are flamboyant. You can easily recognize some of these characteristics in your colleagues, but remember, *they* may have tagged *you* as a good match for a Dilbert character.

Homer Simpson, a dedicated working man from Fox TV, was responding on one show to someone's snide comment about his wearing short sleeves. "What's wrong with that?" said Homer. "Andy Sipowicz wears them all the time." A police detective on TV's *NYPD Blue*, Andy is an interesting choice for an image role model.

When in Rome . . .

How oddly he is suited? I think he bought his doublet
in Italy, his round hose in France, his bonnet in
Germany, and his behavior everywhere.

Portia (describing a suitor), *The Merchant of Venice*, 1, 2

Have you ever gone to an event where you were dressed differently from everybody else? Makes you feel awkward, doesn't it? While still in the courtship phase I invited my wife-to-be to an "Academy Awards" party, for which we were to come dressed as our favorite actors. We arrived at the hotel appropriately garbed—she as Benji, a doggie, and I as Neville Brand, a villainous cowboy—to find we were the only ones in costume. It took a couple of phone calls for us to realize the party was in a different hotel. Did you ever feel like an idiot in public?

Some years back I had crossed the Atlantic as a guest lecturer aboard the QEII. Upon arriving at my hotel in London, I discovered my conservative business suit had a rip in the shoulder. The concierge sent it out for repair, leaving me with my after-hours, somewhat flashy sport jacket. The next day I went over to the London Business School for a meeting. About fifty executives from British companies were there, all dressed in very conservative business suits, and I in my sport jacket. "Ahem," I wanted to say. "I really do know better, but my regular suit is out for repair. I'm not the uncivilized dolt from the colonies you suspect I am!"

> You lisp and wear strange suits.
>
> Rosalind, *As You Like It*. 4, 1

A team pursuing a business opportunity in Hawaii worked hard to prepare for the meeting with several key members of the local agency letting the contract. Said one, "We walked into the room, wearing our standard business dark suits, and instantly realized we'd goofed. Everybody else in the room was casually dressed in Hawaiian style. It was clear we hadn't sized up our audience at all; in fact, it never occurred to us to wear anything other than our normal business wardrobe. Big mistake, as they never warmed up to us."

> A sorry sight.
>
> Macbeth, *Macbeth*. 2, 2

For another Honolulu meeting, our team did opt for Hawaiian shirts, with our on-site rep insisting that he, not we mainlanders, would buy the shirts. Don't know why—I'd seen some great Hawaiian shirts at the 99 store in Detroit.

Appearance Can Even Alienate

> She vaunted 'mongst her minions t' other day
> The very train of her worst wearing gown
> Was better worth than all my father's lands . . .
>
> Queen, *Henry VI, Part 2.* 1, 3

The Queen, predisposed against the Duchess, has been given ammunition to reinforce the intensity of that dislike. Recall Polonius's opening advice: "Rich, not gaudy."

> But I remember when the fight was done,
> When I was dry with rage and extreme toil,
> Breathless and faint, leaning upon my sword,
> Came there a certain lord, neat and trimly dress'd,
> Fresh as a bridegroom; and his chin new reap'd
> Show'd like a stubble-land at harvest-home.
> He was perfumed like a milliner,
> And 'twixt his finger and his thumb he held
> A pouncet-box, which ever and anon
> He gave his nose and took't away again.
>
> Hotspur, *Henry IV, Part 1.* 1, 3

Hotspur, the hard-fighting warrior, is telling of the impression this "certain lord," the king's emissary, made when he showed up to make demands. Dress, timing, attitude, and message all combined to defeat the emissary's goal.

In your work environment, have you seen any examples where appearance or image set back the cause? Here are a couple.

* An executive came before a review committee that would select the winning firm from several bidders. He was immaculately attired in a double-breasted suit of high fashion and $500 Italian shoes, his $10,000 gold watch on prominent display. The reviewers were all mid-level salaried managers and professionals, who could not help but be struck with this wardrobe, clearly out of their budget range.

* For a different competition, an executive drove up in a late-model Mercedes, which was noted by the Plymouth-driving reviewers. (Another fellow arrived by plane for such a meeting, and the car rental agency gave him a Cadillac instead of the usual mid-size vehicle. He returned it, saying, "I didn't want to tick off those people by showing up in a car that fancy.")

Take-Away Ideas

* Make sure your appearance carries a positive message.
* Look better, feel better.
* Suit the wardrobe to the occasion.
* Cut appearance detractors, which can defeat your purpose.

Chapter 9

Get into a Winning State of Mind

All things are ready, if our minds be so.

King Henry. *Henry V.*, 4, 3

Since I have received command to do this business
I have not slept one wink.

Pisanio, *Cymbeline.* 3, 4

Shakespeare had many of his characters engage in self-perusal as they considered various courses of action. Hamlet's "To be or not to be" monologue is a prime example. As a communicator, positive self-talk can be beneficial, while negative self-talk can be defeating. Your mental readiness (or lack thereof) can be a factor in many communication situations, such as interviews (no kidding!), serving as meeting leader, giving testimony, conducting a training session, and—surprise—public speaking.

Nervous? Who, Me?

The sense of death is most in apprehension.

Isabella, *Measure for Measure.* 3, 1

Perhaps you're not real keen about an upcoming encounter. Do you find yourself waking up in the middle of the night with bad thoughts surging through your brain? As you research the situation and prepare your materials, do you get that gnawing feeling of impending doom?

Or perhaps you're in the conference room while an important discussion is going on. You have a contribution you think would be valuable, or you want to ask a question. Your pulse starts to rise, your heart starts thumping, and you suddenly have trouble breathing. You don't put up your hand, and you retreat to the role of passive observer, with the rationalization that you'll speak up later.

The Lion's Den Awaits

. . . the time, the place, the torture.

Lodovico, *Othello*. 5, 2

. . . with fear and trembling.

Leonato, *Much Ado About Nothing*. 2, 3

As you picture yourself walking into that room, do the butterflies start to flutter in your innards? If so, you're not alone. I've asked seminar attendees to free-associate with the word "meetings." Typical responses are

* "It's time for the weekly feeding frenzy."
* "The sharks are circling, and I'm the bait."
* "I feel like Daniel walking into the lions' den."

Distill'd almost to jelly with the act of fear.

Horatio, *Hamlet*. 1, 2

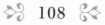

Communication anxiety can be present regardless of one's level of experience. I've worked with senior vice presidents, loaded with assurance, rehearsing for a "must-win" presentation, their notes noticeably shaking. In similar situations, people have ended up at the emergency room as their high-level anxiety activated ulcers or kidney stones.

Some public figures have had to work hard to overcome their severe anxieties about personal appearance or interviews, including Barbra Streisand, Carly Simon, even cocky old James Cagney (who used to keep a bucket handy just offstage; wonder what that was for?)

Remember Albert Brooks as the novice reporter in *Broadcast News*? When his big moment came—the first time on camera with a live newscast—he was frozen speechless, and the sweat poured down from his forehead.

A real broadcaster, *20/20*'s John Stossel, was frustrated as a youth with a stuttering problem. He still works at it, but clearly overcame that difficulty. You're not alone.

> . . . death by inches.
>
> Messenger, *Coriolanus*. 5, 4

I've conducted hundreds of presentations and speeches, yet I have a recurring dream of being in front of an audience and messing up. I'm hung up on some point and can't extricate myself, or something goes wrong with the equipment and trying to get it fixed is an endless, fruitless process. Other experienced speakers and trainers have said that they have similar dreams.

Can Anxiety Work for You?

> Doomsday is near. Die all, die merrily.
>
> Hotspur, *Henry IV, Part 1*. 4, 1

So if anxiety comes with the territory, is that a problem? It can be, if it is severe enough to interfere with your mindset or preparation. Typically, our reaction to the things we don't like to do or find upsetting is to avoid doing them. Procrastination leads to being inadequately prepared, which leads to a poor engagement and outcome, thus validating the initial concern that disaster lies ahead. This is a bad circle to find yourself in, as it infects your next potential opportunity.

> As an unperfect actor on the stage,
> Who with his fear is put besides his part . . .
>
> Sonnet 23

There may be a key identified here. While anxiety is common for different levels of experience, it is probably less for those who have worked to overcome this fear by getting better at their trade, getting past the "unperfect actor" level.

> To fear the worst oft cures the worse.
>
> Cressida, *Troilus and Cressida*. 3, 2

Think of the worst thing that can happen. How bad is that?

Let Your Mind Make Your Body Rich

> For 'tis the mind that makes the body rich.
>
> Petruchio, *The Taming of the Shrew*. 4, 3

Much anxiety is self-generated, as your brain sends negative thoughts and raises a host of "what ifs." "What if I mess up?" "What if I freeze?" "What if they don't pay attention?" "What if they ask me tough questions?"

MACBETH   If we should fail?

LADY M   We fail!
But screw your courage to the sticking-place,
And we'll not fail.

Macbeth. 1, 7

It sometimes helps to consider the question, What will happen to me if I blow it somehow? Usually, the consequences are not as severe as your mind has foretold. They won't have you flogged, boiled in oil, or placed in stocks for public humiliation. Yes, failing is a possibility, but you've taken out insurance by careful preparation. So you might as well head on in there, and the odds are very good "we'll not fail." In the 1984 debates, Democratic vice-presidential candidate Geraldine Ferraro, less experienced at this level of debate than her opponent, was asked about being afraid. Her response used Lady Macbeth's quote (she commented also that this was similar to when she headed into the operating room to have her first baby—no choice but to go in and deliver).

For there is nothing either good or bad but thinking
    makes it so.

Hamlet, *Hamlet.* 2, 2

Through training, careful preparation, practice, and positive self-talk, speakers can replace the "what-ifs" with "Let me at 'em!" I've seen it happen many times. With good results, a new attitude sets in as success builds on success. Many times the person we were so worried about comes through for the actual event. Why? Preparation.

For courage mounteth with occasion.
Let them be welcome then; we are prepared.

Austria, *King John.* 2, 1

Many have found visualization to be helpful in creating a positive state of mind. Close your eyes and picture in detail the setting for the engagement ahead. See the room, the audience members sitting across the table, the audiovisual gear in action and clearly showing your important slides. Imagine yourself communicating a concept, and see the positive audience reactions: the heads nodding in understanding, the high level of interest as they lean forward to hear your words, and finally the loud "huzzahs" and standing ovation. (That may be stretching it for your upcoming assignment to lead the departmental safety meeting, but you never know.)

The nerves can start working overtime as the occasion draws near. So what can you do to get them back to a manageable level? Say you're sitting at the conference table and are considering speaking up.

* Tighten your toes and hold it for 10 seconds. (Bruce Willis passed on similar advice in the movie *Die Hard*—oops—forget that title.)

* Take a breath in, not by puffing out your chest but filling your diaphragm. Put a hand on your stomach to feel it move out. Hold that for a few seconds, then s-l-o-w-l-y exhale. Think about blowing on a candle but not putting it out. Try that again.

* Jot down a planned comment or question onto a notepad or card. Think about the phrasing.

* Cough lightly or take a sip of water to clear the vocal cords.

* Make your entry with a firm word, raised hand, or request of the meeting chairperson.

* Start speaking with projection to all.

The Babbling Dreams Make Their 3 A.M. Appearance

Let not our babbling dreams affright our souls.

Richard, Richard III. 5, 3

Tomorrow's the day. It will be your time in the spotlight, whether you have to run an important meeting, march in and ask the boss for a raise, or give a status report (especially with bad news). So to bed with all things ready.

You've prepared thoroughly, perhaps for days. Your brain is on overload, and the tension mounts. You wake up in the middle of the night with numbers and charts and perhaps, as in *Rape of Lucrece*, with "wolve's death-boding cries" racing through your mind. It happens.

> How many thousands of my poorest subjects
> Are at this hour asleep! O sleep, O gentle sleep,
> Nature's soft nurse, how have I frighted thee,
> That thou no more wilt weigh my eyelids down
> And steep my senses in forgetfulness? . . .
> Uneasy lies the head that wears a crown.

King Henry, Henry IV, Part 2. 3, 1

Even kings and CEOs can have trouble keeping the job from interfering with their gentle sleep.

Fitted for Drink? Not Right Now, Please

BARNARDINE   I have been drinking all night; I am not fitted for 't.

POMPEY   O, the better, sir; for he that drinks all night, and
is hanged betimes in the morning, may sleep the
sounder all the next day.

Measure for Measure. 4, 3

With zero hour approaching, the nerves may still be working over-time and your pulse rate is moving upward. At this point, some people follow the advice of well-meaning friends: "Relax. Have a martini or two. That will calm your nerves and loosen you up." Resist that bad advice (and examine Pompey's logic before buying into it).

I have very poor and unhappy brains for drinking: I
would well wish courtesy would invent some other
custom of entertainment.

Cassio, *Othello.* 2, 3

It sometimes happens that the one or two drinks turn into three or four, and disaster lurks. Many people have embarrassed themselves by showing up clearly overindulged, with slurred speech, mumbling, dropped notes, and forgotten lines as evidence. Want to make the headlines at Hollywood's Oscars night? Give your acceptance speech while clearly soused. Works every time.

Watch the Onions and Garlic

And most dear actors, eat no onions nor garlic, for we
are to utter sweet breath.

Bottom, *A Midsummer Night's Dream.* 4, 2

For that extra confidence edge, a bit more attention to detail is in order.

> Bid them wash their faces,
> And keep their teeth clean.
>
> Coriolanus, *Coriolanus*. 2, 3

You want to be certain that bad breath, body odor, unkempt hair, floppy hose, or a gurgling stomach doesn't kill the deal. Hmmm—do those audience snickers mean a key button or zipper is open?

You're on—Charge!

> Up, princes! and, with spirit of honor edged
> More sharper than your swords, hie to the field.
>
> King of France, *Henry V.* 3, 5

Showtime has arrived, so take a few deep breaths, put yourself into a positive frame of mind, and head into that conference room like you owned the place. To borrow the title of the book by John Weitz, adopt the attitude of the *Man* (or Woman)-*in-Charge*.

> Once more unto the breach, dear friends, once more;
> Or close the wall up with our English dead.
> In peace there's nothing so becomes a man
> As modest stillness and humility:
> But when the blast of war blows in our ears,
> Then imitate the action of the tiger;
> Stiffen the sinews, summon up the blood.
>
> Henry, *Henry V.* 3, 1

Take-Away Ideas

* A positive state of mind is a valuable asset.
* Manage your anxiety.
* Get plenty of rest when an important engagement is ahead.
* Take care of the personal details.
* Go in with an attitude of success.

Part III

> ⤜❧⤛

The Receiver and Feedback Roles

Twelfth-Night; or, What You Will. 2, 3

So far most of our focus has been on the sender of information. Yet in communication, there's another party involved: the receiver of information. That may be a person on the other end of a phone or across a desk, a group of people in a meeting, or perhaps several people linked via a phone, video, or Internet conference. Some of the information interchange may occur sequentially: that is, you send for awhile, and the other person listens and then responds. Or it may be a continuous two-way discussion. For successful two-way interchange, be aware of positive or detrimental outcomes from (1) your sending *style, (2) your* receiving *behavior; (3) your ability to give* feedback. *Part III examines these skills and behaviors.*

Chapter 10

⤜≫⁕≪⤛

Bestow the Sense of . . . Hey There, Are You Listening?

Sweet royalty, bestow on me the sense of hearing.

Armado, *Love's Labour's Lost*. 5, 2

How many good talkers do you know? How many good listeners? Probably your answers show that truly good listeners are harder to find than good talkers. Yet experience probably reveals that you value good listeners, especially since they don't interrupt you when you're on a vocalizing roll. This suggests that becoming a better communicator means taking a look at your own listening style.

How's Your *Sense of Hearing?*

CHIEF JUSTICE   You hear not what I say to you.

FALSTAFF   Very well, my lord, very well: rather an't please you, it is the disease of not listening, the malady of not marking that I am troubled withal.

CHIEF JUSTICE   To punish you by the heels would amend the attention of your ears.

Henry IV, Part 2. 1, 2

It pays for any organization to keep lines of communication open so that important information is allowed and encouraged to surface. What's the reality? Former Chrysler president Lynn Townsend said, "Perhaps the most common deficiency in corporate communications today is an inadequate upward flow of information. . . . An employee is often reluctant to give his or her boss the bad news. And poor listening habits by individual managers frequently discourage subordinates. If the boss is not a good listener, those who report to him will soon stop trying to communicate with him."

Speaking up has proven to be sometimes dangerous to one's career, as some "whistle blowers" reporting shoddy practices have found out. Employees typically blow the whistle because they've been frustrated by getting no action through the organization's internal communications systems. (That lack of actual or perceived response happens to be why my position of ombudsman was established.) Several who have gone public internally or externally have found themselves shunted off to less desirable jobs or even been fired. This sort of reception seems bound to stifle free flow of information, although some have successfully gone to court to regain those jobs.

The most famous space program failure, the blow-up following liftoff of the Space Shuttle *Challenger*, has been examined in crucial detail. The findings showed that the rocket company's technical team reported the high potential of a failure due to launch conditions. Higher leadership gave inadequate attention to this input and went ahead with the launch, with the resulting setback to the entire manned space program.

Are You a Good Listener?

Give every man thy ear, but few thy voice.

Polonius, *Hamlet*. 1, 3

Books abound on the topic of how to become a better listener. Seminars are regularly offered to help people understand their own listening flaws and ways to correct them. A common response from graduates of such programs is "You know who really ought to attend this seminar?" Everybody knows one or two lousy listeners. And maybe some good ones.

Is listening important in business? Here's one indicator. The Society for Marketing Professional Services asked 150 firms what attributes they valued in choosing among competitors for design and construction projects. Respondents said that "personal chemistry," a hard-to-define term, frequently was the winning difference. Per one respondent, "Honesty, responsiveness and *good listening skills* won out over 'overt sucking up.' "

In 1972, Norman Mailer wrote that Democratic presidential nominee George McGovern was lacking in charisma. Then Mailer met McGovern at an event and started relaying to the candidate his impressions of the convention speeches: "And McGovern listened with that charisma which was finally and indisputably his own—which was to listen—for if his voice had no flaming tongue of fire, his power to listen surrounded everyone who spoke in his presence, and had the depth to capture many a loyalty before he was done."

Around that time I was also a candidate for public office, a few levels down from the senator. At one event, I was discussing politics with a state senator. During our brief conversation, he kept looking past me, presumably to locate someone (anyone?) more interesting than I. Perhaps he caught 2 percent of what I said, which was, of course, witty, with flashes of brilliant insight, and certainly invaluable. I voted against him next time he ran—taught him a lesson. (OK, he won, and I didn't, so the point again is . . . ?)

Here's a quick test of how good a listener you are. Remember that meeting you attended where you were introduced to several new people? How many names could you recall one minute later? *Tip*:

Repeat it aloud immediately, and then, as soon as possible, write it down on a notecard.

The primary listening flaw is—surprise, not listening. We pay lip service (if that's a fitting metaphor) to listening. The other person starts talking and we start listening, except our minds take us elsewhere. (What was her name again?. . . . starting to rain outside. . . . look at that funny tie . . . yes, that reminds me of something I want to say . . . ooo, that salsa was hot . . . hmmm, did I lock the car?) "Yes, yes, I'm listening."

Dr. Carl Rogers developed a valuable exercise for testing if we truly are attending or listening. Set a topic for discussion. One person talks, the other listens. Then, before the second person can make a statement, he or she must repeat back what the first person said, to that person's agreement. I've used this simple drill in classes; it is not easy, especially if the topic is one for which the two parties have opposing views.

Also enlightening is the old chain communication exercise, where the first person whispers a simple message to the second person. The message might start as "We'll meet at 2:00 in Jan's office to finalize plans for our trip to Washington." That is passed on to the third person and it continues along to the last person. Try this without feedback, and it's likely to end up as "Washington bureaucrats, who met until 2 A.M. in Jan's bar, have wiped out our plans." Now try the same process, allowing participants to discuss the message with the previous person, and the result will be close to what started out.

Thus, when conveying information or directions, take that extra 20 seconds and ask your associate to repeat back what they think you said. When receiving, repeat back to the sender what you heard. (Sender: hold your impatience, let the person talk.) This little tip can head off mistakes and save later embarrassment.

In communication training programs, role plays between supervisor and subordinate are valuable for improving counseling and coaching skills. Good outcomes almost always occur when there is an even balance of talking or when the supervisor listens more than talks. The outcome is generally poor when the supervisor dominates the conversation, sometimes doing up to 80 percent of the talking.

Do You Let Others Tell Their Tales?

It is not well done, mark you now, to take the tales out of my mouth ere it is made and finished.

Fluellen, Henry V. 4, 7

Nathan Miller said "Conversation in the U.S. is a competitive exercise in which the first person to draw a breath is declared the listener."

CELIA   Give me audience, good madam.

ROSALIND   Proceed.

CELIA   There lay he stretched along, like a wounded knight.

ROSALIND   Though it be pity to see such a sight, it well becomes the ground.

CELIA   Cry "Holla" to thy tongue, I prithee; it curvets unseasonably. He was furnished like a hunter.

ROSALIND   O, ominous! he comes to kill my heart.

CELIA   I would sing my song without a burden. Thou bringest me out of tune.

As You Like It. 3, 2

Do you know someone who regularly interrupts people as they are trying to talk? Or who finishes your sentences before you do? Not too aggravating, is it? Now check your own dialogue practice—maybe you do a lot of interrupting that others find irritating. I know it's highly unlikely, but check.

Paul Sullivan of the international consulting firm Global Partners notes a problem that characterizes many conversations. He said many people don't engage in dialogue at all. "Somebody coined a phrase which better fits the way many of us communicate—duo-logue, where both parties talk, neither listens, so the messages don't ever go into the ears, but instead pass by each other. Sometimes it's even one step further, and becomes a duel-logue."

Monty Python applied this technique in one of their skits, which goes roughly like this:

"Did not!"
"Did so!"
"Did not!"
"Yes I did!"
Ad infinitum.

What's Your Response Style?

PRINCESS   No, to the death we will not move a foot:
Nor to their penn'd speech render we no grace;
But while 'tis spoke each turn away her face.

BOYET   Why, that contempt will kill the speaker's heart,
And quite divorce his memory from his part.

Love's Labour's Lost. 5, 2

As a receiver, your nonverbal manner of listening can affect the sender—sometimes in a helpful manner, sometimes not. Put yourself into the role of speaker. Do you enjoy talking to a stone-faced, tight-mouthed, barely reactive listener? Or is it more comfortable if the receiver shows some interest, perhaps even encouragement? Watch the TV cop shows when they're grilling suspects to see how they use their response style to affect and uncover the bad guys.

In the receiver role you can do much to help facilitate communication or defeat it. Many organizations tout their open-door policies, which can lead to a lot of traffic with the right environment and minimal barriers. Other "open doors" appear well guarded, with a watchdog, an intimidating office setup, and a desk/seating layout that says, "I'm the boss and don't you forget it." A master at anticommunication was Major Major, played unforgettably by Bob Newhart, in the movie *Catch 22*. Whenever he was about to get surly visitors, he would flee the scene by jumping out the window. Haven't you had that urge sometimes?

Assuming that a connection has occurred, by clearly paying attention, giving eye contact, and responding by nodding (not off), smiling, or even frowning, you give clues to the sender. Such body language showing a genuine interest can help a nervous subordinate or associate.

MACBETH   Your royal father's murder'd.

MALCOLM   O, by whom?

Macbeth. 2, 3

Doesn't this reaction to terrible news seem strange, even incongruous? Unless there's some emotional content in these lines, the sender will be puzzled at the muted comment, perhaps even assuming Malcolm expected this to occur, and maybe even had a hand in it. None of that may be true, but the fact of the combined spoken and nonspoken response not matching the reality raises these issues.

In communication across cultures, the receiver's natural responses may be much different from your own; this can create confusion and possible discomfort. I recall a trip to India where I was engaging in dialogue with a shopkeeper. I was frequently confused when he would say "yes" and his head shaking, to me, said "no."

125

Respond to Facilitate, Not Dominate

Every one can master a grief but he that has it.

Benedick, *Much Ado About Nothing*. 3.2

When a friend or colleague is sending a message, such as "I'm fed up with this place and all the useless junk that keeps a person from doing their job!" how do you respond? Do you truly listen, or does your part of the dialogue sound like this? "I know just how you feel . . . That reminds me of something that happened to me; let me tell you . . . Oh, you're making a big deal out of nothing . . . Remember, out of adversity often comes strength . . . What you need to do is . . . Grow up!"

Reading these words on a page, you probably sense they would not do much to further the dialogue. Yet don't you know someone who responds about like that? (Someone else, of course, not you.)

The problem with these responses is they put down or discount the sender, whether or not that is the intention. The receiver has instantly taken over as being wiser than the sender. And in doing so, he or she (1) fails to truly hear what the sender is saying or feeling, and (2) inhibits, not helps, the communication.

Go back and review those earlier responses, and consider the effect they would have on you, had you been the original sender. What might be better responses to that colleague's lament? As a company ombudsman, I found I needed to review my old standard response patterns to be effective. Here are some of the tips that worked, as adapted from *People Skills* by Robert Bolton:

* Give them your attention. Put down the paper you're reading. Look at them, not the computer screen. Use the

"mute" button. If you can't give them your attention now, say so and set a later time.

* Truly absorb what they are saying, even if it sounds, to you, trivial, stupid, and irrational. It isn't to them.

* Don't be a sphinx. Show your interest as they speak, with a nod or "hmmm," or "That's interesting." Sincerely want to hear what's on their mind, meaning watch for your sneers, smug facial expression, or rolling eyeballs. (Remember how those got Al Gore into trouble?)

* Withhold instant judgment. Keep yourself out of it, at least for awhile.

* Go with the flow, at least initially, and encourage it. If emotions are running high, those generally need to be dealt with before you go into analysis mode. Help them vent, and better appreciate what's going on with expressions such as "Sounds serious," "Wow, you're really steamed,"or "Something triggered your hot button." By respecting their feelings, your nonjudgmental responses—Bolton terms this "reflective listening"—are likely to keep the flow going.

* Help them clarify by asking for specifics. "What happened?" "I'm not sure I understand; can you give me an example?" These may elicit useful information.

* Help them examine the situation and, if appropriate, work together toward a resolution. If they only have part of the story, you can provide a fuller context. If another party is involved, you may want to hear the other side of the issue. (I found this especially important as an ombudsman.) Ask for their solutions before offering yours. "What do you suggest?" will probably be more useful than your "You know what you should do? Blah, blah, blah . . ."

Are You a Spendthrift of Your Tongue?

> Fie, what a spendthrift is he of his tongue!
>
> Antonio, *The Tempest.* 2, 1

When in dialogue mode, it's easy to become absorbed with what *you* want to say. It's not a bad idea to check from time to time if the other party to the communication is still interested in what you have to say.

> I cried "Hum," and "Well, go to!"
> But marked him not a word. O, he is as tedious
> As a tired horse, a railing wife,
> Worse than a smoky house.
>
> Hotspur, *Henry IV, Part 1.* 3, 1

While I'm sure you, yourself, would never be guilty of overtalking, you probably know someone else who is guilty of it. That's the person who stops by your desk for a brief chat, starting with "How are *you*?" and then proceeding to tell in painful detail, for the next 20 minutes, how *they* are. The one who calls with a quick hello, with the rest of the discussion spent by them talking and you listening, sort of, while catching up on your mail, polishing your nails, or watching TV. (*Point of interest:* Hotspur, who lodged the complaint against Glendower, was notorious for talking and not listening.)

As a Sender, Be Alert for Audience "Toothaches"

> 'Tis a very excellent piece of work, madame lady:
>   would 'twere done.
>
> Christopher Sly, *The Taming of the Shrew.* 1, 1

For there was never yet philosopher
That could endure the toothache patiently.

Leonato, Much Ado About Nothing. 5, 1

"Oh, is that ever true," you probably say, "but how can I use that in business communication?" Have you ever experienced a shift in your key listeners' attention? Good senders are constantly in tune with their communication partners. When internal or external "toothaches"—pressing problems, meeting conflicts, notes slipped to the CEO's attention—distract listeners' attention from the message of the moment, alert presenters size up the situation and adapt as needed.

Speak on; but be not over-tedious.

Burgundy, Henry VI, Part 1. 3, 3

In addition to giving *nonverbal* signals, receivers may flat out tell you it's time to head for the finish line. One of the main problems in communication is misjudging how much information your audience may want. Your colleagues may want to hear all the details, but your boss may not. (This could even be true for communicating with your spouse or, gadzooks, your kids.) The reasons are many: The boss has different information needs; time pressures in a meeting can dictate how much can be allocated to a topic, or your detailed knowledge may be impressive but beyond the grasp of the boss.

More of your conversation would infect my brain.

Menenius, Coriolanus. 2, 1

Some receivers, especially superiors, may not be shy about telling you it's time to wrap it up. Others may find that difficult because (1) you're *their* boss, (2) group pressures may be inhibiting them, or (3) they've been pounced on before under such circumstances. If you're on a verbal roll, keep checking your receivers for those non-verbal indicators: yawns, doodling, frequent watch checking, reading the morning newspaper, hypnotic stares, and so on.

> You cram these words into mine ears against the
> stomach of my sense.
>
> Alonso, *The Tempest.* 2, 1

The signals are coming strong now. This is one fed-up receiver.

> Wilt not a calf's-skin stop that mouth of thine?
>
> Philip the Bastard, *King John.* 3, 1

This communication is about to take a nasty turn, or perhaps an abrupt end, or even a punch in the mouth.

Improving Your Listening (and Relationship) Skills

A good investment is a seminar or after-hours listening class, including one tied to family communication, such as parent effectiveness training. Pick up almost any book on listening. In a nonthreatening way, discuss the topic with others to see how together you can improve listening.

The following are also helpful to listening. As a sender,

* Make sure the receiver is attending to you. If they're reading the paper or a report, they may say, "Yes . . . uh, huh . . . go on . . ." and not be catching anything you're saying. So later when you say, "But I told you that this morning," you'll be right—you sent it, they didn't receive it.

* Check that the medium isn't interfering. Talking with the TV on, with loud office noise, or with many people talking will wipe out much of your message.

* Speak loudly and distinctly as the environment warrants. If you mumble and race, don't be surprised when they don't get it. Repeat if necessary.

* Put feeling into your voice and body language. If it's urgent, make that clear. If it's wonderful, let that come through.

* Check for comprehension in their reaction, especially facial expression. What does a wrinkled brow, squinty eyes, a shoulder shrug, or a snicker tell you?

As a receiver,

* Check your physical environment. Does your office entry, room layout, or seating arrangement facilitate or intimidate those who might want to communicate with you, especially those lower in rank?

* If this is an incoming phone call, common courtesy says to use the handset, not the speaker phone. Want to really upset someone? Take the call, chat for a while, then reveal that six others were listening to every word over the speaker phones. If you do want to use a speaker phone, alert the caller and state who else is tuned in.

* Give the speaker your full attention. Stop reading, take your hands off the keyboard, quit talking to others.

* Fend off mental diversions such as the other person's wardrobe, haircut, physical appearance, or voice. These can send your mind elsewhere and activate prejudices that can cloud the communication.

* Look directly at them, so they know you're with them and

⇨ 131 ⇦

you can pick up more than just the words. Possibly lean toward them, and be attentive, not cavalier.

* Shhhh. Let them finish a thought.

* Wait awhile, and then, if you're not getting it, ask for clarification. If you think you got it, repeat it to make sure.

* Help them by reacting—verbally such as "Go on . . . uh, huh . . . OK . . . Keep going . . ."; nonverbally by nodding, responding naturally, smiling, or head shaking as appropriate.

* Facilitate their sending—they may not be communicating smoothly—by asking for more information. Let them know you're missing out and need more focus, or see if you're getting it right by applying their message to an example.

* Finally, if you're talking with them, talk with them. Unless that incoming phone call is critically important, let the machine answer it. If you have to take the call, explain and ask for a moment's break. If it goes long, indicate that you'll resume the conversation once the call is over. Do it.

* Take notes to help you capture the key points. This can be helpful in phone conversations, reviews, briefings, training sessions, even in one-on-one conversations.

Take-Away Ideas

* Being open to hearing what others have to say is an important attribute.

* Truly listen to what others are saying.

* Respond in a manner that helps senders (unless you don't want to).

* Think in terms of dialogue, not duel-logue.

* As a sender, stay tuned into your audience; are they still with you?

* Be aware of how much your talking dominates conversation; give others a chance also.

* Take a class, buy a book, invest in listening improvement.

Chapter 11

Receiver Meets Sender in Q&A

What wouldst thou have, boor? what, thick-skin? speak,
breathe, discuss; brief, short, quick, snap.

Host, *The Merry Wives of Windsor*. 4, 5

We now shift to the Q&A (question and answer), a major part of
business communications. Similar to a tennis match, the server asks
the questions—the prosecutor in a courtroom, the reporter at a press
conference, the customer who will perhaps buy the services. The
other side returns with, hopefully, useful answers that will benefit the
communication for both parties. Put yourself in both roles, as the
one asking the questions and then as the one who comes up with
the answers.

As Questioner, How's Your Performance?

ROSALIND   What did he do when thou sawest him? What
said he? How looked he? Wherein went he? What
makes he here? Did he ask for me? Where remains he?
How parted he with thee? and when shalt thou see him
again? Answer me in one word.

CELIA   You must first borrow me Gargantua's mouth first;
'tis a word too great for any mouth of this age's size.

As You Like It. 3, 2

This is a tough set of questions to digest, let alone answer. If you are the questioner, take an extra moment to think through your question, even writing it down so that it is clear and workable.

ACHILLES   Tell me, you heavens, in which part of his body
Shall I destroy him? . . . answer me, heavens!

HECTOR   It would discredit the blest gods, proud man,
To answer such a question.

Troilus and Cressida. 4, 5

Wording questions in an attacking manner, even if not consciously intended, can have a discouraging effect. What is your reaction when someone asks you a question starting with the accusatory or blaming word "why"?

* "Why didn't you get that report in on time?" (if you hadn't goofed around . . .)

* "Why did you choose A instead of B?" (obviously a dumb choice)

Or those fault-finding statements posing as questions:

* "What's wrong with you? Can't you ever do it right (idiot)?"

* "Can't you remember to run the spell-checker before you turn in a report? I've told you a dozen times (numbskull). Don't you learn anything (ignoramus)?"

Or the pseudo questions that place the receiver in a no-win situation:

* "Have you stopped beating your spouse?" If they answer yes or no, they lose.

* "Which is it, X or Y?" Maybe it's really Z or XX, but you've pinned the person in (unless he or she knows how to work out of it).

Questions like these almost always make the receiver defensive, perhaps even antagonistic. If this is your typical type of question, check the reactions. Try a less attacking phrasing and see if you get a different response: "Les, the report came in after our deadline. Can you tell me what caused the delay?"

In many competitive bids, the guiding agency sets up specific rules for the sort of questions that will be permitted during reviews (e.g., a clarification question is OK, an argumentative question is not). They then monitor these to ensure that each team gets fair treatment, and to head off possible protests if one bidder perceives that it got beat up and the winner got a soft ride.

In a problem-solving meeting or training session, the leader truly wants to elicit questions. If the environment, physical and interpersonal, is not inviting or safe, questions may not be forthcoming. People don't like to be embarrassed or shot down. I watched a major leadership guru at a seminar solicit questions and then insult the person who asked the question. Sure enough, after the first few questions, only brave souls or masochists rose to try any more. Be aware of your body language in such situations. Your impatient tone of voice, intimidating glare, head shakes, and signs of irritation all signal to others that asking questions here can threaten one's self-worth and possibly career. I recall a supervisor who had just finished his presentation of a new company policy; he stood fully erect with arms tightly crossed in front of his chest, and asked, "Any questions?" Guess what—there weren't any.

Assuming you do want to encourage dialogue, try some of these tips:

* Remove the barriers. Get away from the lectern, and move closer to the audience.

* Have a couple of ice-breaking questions or ticklers ready, such as "One question I'm often asked is . . ." or "You probably have some questions about when the layoffs will start . . ."

* Remove the pressure with activities, such as having people first go over the issue in a quick partner discussion or have a short exercise that puts them in an active verse passive mode.

As Questioner, Do You Kill Off the Messengers?

In any situation, when you are the one asking the questions or receiving information, watch out that you don't shoot the messenger. Few things stifle questions—and potentially valuable input—faster than this. Consider this series of questions between Cleopatra and a messenger with new information about what her true love, Antony, has been up to.

CLEOPATRA   O', from Italy!
Ram thou thy faithful tidings in mine ears,
That long time have been barren.
. . . .
MESSENGER   Madam, he's married to Octavia.

❧ 138 ❧

CLEOPATRA   The most infectious pestilence upon thee!
   (*Strikes him down*)

MESSENGER   Good madam, patience.

CLEOPATRA   . . . Horrible villain! Or I'll spurn thine
   eyes
Like balls before me; I'll unhair thy head.
   (*She hales him up and down*)
Thou shalt be whipp'd with wire, and stew'd in brine,
Smarting in lingering pickle.

MESSENGER   Gracious madam,
I that do bring the news made not the match.

Antony and Cleopatra. 2, 5

The information flow has dried up. Don't let this happen to you or your organization.

In 1969 the Vietnam War was at its height. Cambodian ruler, Prince Sihanouk (who would be deposed within a year), sent a strong message to the U.S. leadership (specially President Nixon and Henry Kissinger). Wrote Seymour Hersh, "But Sihanouk's message was stark: The United States should consider a strategic face-saving retreat. It was too late to save South Vietnam. In the Nixon-Kissinger White House, the messenger carrying bad news was always beheaded."

As Responder, Do You Vanish or Shine in Q&A?

When I burned in desire to question them further, they
made themselves into air, into which they vanished.

Lady Macbeth, *Macbeth*. 1, 5

Many people have a dim view of the Q&A part of engagements. Their hope is to escape with no questions. They approach events with a fear of having someone bore in on them, making them look foolish.

A much wiser attitude is to welcome Q&A, even to seek it out as an opportunity to (1) clear up misunderstandings, (2) provide added information, (3) assess acceptance or disagreement, and (4) find information you can use. In preparing your communications, prepare for Q&A as well.

> Ask me what question thou canst possible,
> And I will answer unpremeditated.
>
> Pucelle (Joan of Arc), *Henry VI, Part 1*. 1, 2

In many engagements, how well you handle the Q&A can be more important than the formal prepared message you have conveyed. Poor responses to questions in interviews or debates have seriously set back political campaigns (e.g., those of Gerald Ford, Ted Kennedy, and Michael Dukakis, and strong responses have advanced others (John Kennedy, Ronald Reagan, Bill Clinton, John McCain).

Good responses to questions can make or break your chances in many situations, such as job interviews, critical reviews, or venture capital engagements. In a proposal review, a team blew one critical question, serious enough it cost them the contract; another, headed for a loss, pulled it out in the Q&A.

In Q&A, Being Cute Rarely Works

HAMLET   What man dost thou dig it [a grave] for?

CLOWN   For no man, sir.

HAMLET   What woman then?

❧ 140 ❧

CLOWN   For none, neither.

HAMLET   Who is to be buried in 't?

CLOWN   One that was a woman, sir; but, rest her soul,
she's dead.

HAMLET   How absolute the knave is! we must speak by the
card, or equivocation will undo us.

Hamlet. 5, 1

While this exchange is highly entertaining on stage, you can see that
Hamlet is getting more agitated with each response. The clown is
responding to each question with a totally literal (and amusing, to
him) answer, but it's infuriating to the questioner, who is trying to
get information. When this sort of dialogue occurs in the business
world, someone's career is probably about to be impacted.

BIRON   Did I not dance with you in Brabant once?

ROSALINE   Did I not dance with you in Brabant once?

BIRON   I know you did.

ROSALINE   How needless was it, then, to ask the question!

BIRON   You must not be so quick.

ROSALINE   'Tis long of you that spur me with such
questions.

Love's Labour's Lost. 2, 1

As this Q&A progresses, both sides are getting progressively more
aggravated. Part of this comes from the spoken words, the rest from
how things are said.

Watch the tendency toward defensiveness, a common reaction
when the question seems challenging. In a practice session, a manager
who was asked a somewhat challenging question immediately went

on the attack. The next question was more challenging. The battle escalated. Soon a couple of others joined in as part of the grilling team, and they were getting downright nasty. I blew the whistle, and we reviewed the video of this exchange. The receiver thought he'd done well—"I showed 'em, didn't I?" However he'd lost his objective, and a lot of goodwill. He defined his approach to Q&A: "I respond to them with the same manner they ask me the questions." Made him feel good, except he lost the war he'd created.

Nonverbal messages provide strong signals that can create problems for responders. You provide the likely tone of voice, facial expression, eye movement for the following comments and predict what reaction will be created in those stupid audience members:

* "I already explained that."

* "Not again!"

* "How many times do I have to explain this?"

* "If you'll just hold it, I'm coming to that."

Sometimes people get defensive when a question comes their way, not realizing that the sender is truly trying to help them. The sender may know the answer, but realizes that (a) you didn't explain it well or (b) a colleague isn't fully understanding your story, so the sender is giving you a golden opportunity to explain it in more detail so the colleague can get it.

For Success, Be Ready

GUILDENSTERN   If it shall please you to make me a
    wholesome (intelligent) answer, I will do your mother's
    commandment . . .

HAMLET   Sir, I cannot.

ROSENCRANTZ   What, my lord?

HAMLET   Give you a wholesome answer; my wit's diseased.

Hamlet. 3, 2

It appears Hamlet was not prepared for this phase of the discussion (though he's actually deliberately dodging).

JAQUES   Can you nominate in order now the degrees of the lie?

TOUCHSTONE   O, sir, we quarrel in print, by the book; as you have books for good manners. I will name you the degrees. The first, the Retort Courteous; the second, the Quip Modest; the third, the Reply Churlish; the fourth, the Reproof Valiant; the fifth, the Countercheck Quarrelsome; the sixth, the Lie with Circumstance; the seventh, the Lie Direct.

As You Like It. 5, 4

In contrast, Touchstone seems to have been totally ready for that question. In getting ready for a successful Q&A, think of potential questions this audience might ask. Then research and try out your answers to those questions. Get some feedback about the quality of your answers and the manner in which you provide them. Do this for upcoming interviews, staff meetings (especially if the content is contentious), presentations, testimonies, and court appearances.

This is the process presidential candidates use in preparing for press conferences and debates. Attorneys prepare witnesses this way. In preparing for major presentations, I provide specific training for Q&A and then drill the team with likely questions. In these simulations, the team almost always does poorly the first time, but with more practice the responses and teamwork improve.

Some other tips for surviving (and thriving) in Q&A:

* If you don't understand the question, rather than ask the person to repeat it, take the burden on yourself and paraphrase the question: "Let me make sure I understand the question. What you want to know is . . ." This can also be helpful for making sure you actually do understand it and can buy you some time to think before answering.

* Take a moment to think about your answer before spouting off, and instantly regretting it.

* Answer the question concisely, rather than wander around it. (Politicians are often skilled at avoiding the true question, a technique that doesn't go far with senior management or customers.)

* If you don't know the answer, (1) admit it, *and offer to get the information;* (2) refer the question to a colleague (it's good if he or she were listening); (3) ask if anyone else, including the questioner, has some input.

Take-Away Ideas

* The Q&A interchange can be an important part of communication and can help or hinder desired results.

* As questioner, take your role seriously and think before asking questions.

* As responder, prepare for answering questions.

* Be aware of how spoken and nonspoken messages can influence how well your answers are received.

 144

Chapter 12

Test the Verbosity to the Argument: Sharpen Your Critical Listening Skill

> Here comes a flattering rascal.
>
> Queen, *Cymbeline*. 1, 5

A big part of the receiver's role is deciding whether the speaker's case is sound and worth pursuing, or unsound and to be rejected. This is useful when the telemarketer or financial hawker calls with an offer too good to be true. In business this can be part of a one-on-one dialogue or a meeting called to decide on a course of action. It may be inherent in the process, as for negotiations or job interviews. Or it can be specifically structured, as for a proposal evaluation, venture capital forum, or academic review.

Look Beyond the Sugar'd Words

> Your grace attended to their sugar'd words,
> But look'd not on the poison of their hearts.
>
> Gloucester, *Richard III*. 3, 1

The speaker was first-rate. He spoke with assurance about the wisdom of the proposed investment. He dressed for success. The room was in a respected hotel, and the breakfast was fine. His slides were top-quality and clearly displayed the key information we needed to make a sound decision. He had the backing of a major financial firm. He welcomed and responded to any concerns the audience had. He asked for the order, and I responded with a check.

Great presentation, bad decision. I plead guilty to not applying critical listening, as this proved to be a terrible investment, most of it disappearing within a year. Was I exposed to a "flattering rascal," or was it a matter of bad timing or inadequate investigation? Maybe a little of each. But above all, I failed to take responsibility for being an astute receiver and reviewer.

Does the Argument Hold?

He draweth out the thread of his verbosity finer than
the staple of his argument.

Holofernes, *Love's Labour's Lost.* 5, 1

We have ample examples in life and fiction of characters plying their wares with sincerity, fervor, and righteousness. Shakespeare's Iago successfully applied his sinister stratagems on Othello, a lost cause in the critical listening category. Other masters include snake oil salesmen of the old West, P. T. Barnum with his "A sucker's born every minute" slogan, the Music Man with all his promises and no action, and—always with us—boiler room investment scams.

We're regularly exposed to carefully choreographed pitches:

* "Guaranteed 50 percent returns"
* "The clearly superior deal of a lifetime"

* "The long-distance phone service that beats all competitors"
* "No-strings free trip to Hawaii"

As is often said, if it sounds too good to be true, it probably is.

Keep Your Flim-Flam Detector on Alert

> Gratiano speaks an infinite deal of nothing, more than
> any man in Venice. His reasons are as two grains of
> wheat hid in two bushels of chaff: you shall seek all
> day ere you find them: and when you have them,
> they are not worth the search.
>
> Bassanio, *The Merchant of Venice*. 1, 1

In the movie *The Flim-Flam Man*, George C. Scott portrayed a master at conning others with phrases, style, and deep sincerity—all phony, that is. Someone coined a useful phrase for listeners, "crap detector," an internal warning system that would go on alert and spot the baloney coming your way. An astute reviewer, looks past the outside layer of smooth delivery and snappy computer-based graphics and into the clarity of ideas, the accuracy of support, the soundness of propositions, and the proven competency of the players.

> Mere prattle without practice.
>
> Iago, *Othello*. 1, 1

It's easy to make claims, harder to validate that they've proven successful in application. Ask for the proof, and check the legitimacy. As President Reagan reminded Premier Gorbachev during critical arms negotiations, borrowing from an old axiom, "Trust . . . and verify."

> I am well acquainted with your manner of wrenching
>   the true cause the false way.
>
> Chief Justice, *Henry IV, Part* 2. 2, 1

Those conveying information may not be intentionally misleading the receivers; maybe they had a weak case, didn't prepare adequately, missed key information, or lacked expertise. Others indeed may be covering up key information, playing loosely with facts, or deliberately lying. We've seen ample examples of these via some sensational Congressional investigations.

> And now, instead of bullets wrapp'd in fire,
> To make a shaking fever in your walls,
> They shoot but calm words folded up in smoke,
> To make a faithless error of your ears.
>
> King John, *King John.* 2, 1

Put another way, there are some out there who use slick words, conveying that all is well, to cloud reality, where all may be lousy. Your challenge is to make sure decisions are based on good information. How good is your ability to do that?

* Have you prepared adequately by researching the topic under discussion? Reviewed advance information?

* Do you have adequate resources to complement your own background?

* Have you set your own criteria for assessing the effectiveness of the various approaches? (In competitive procurements the reviewers typically set specific evaluation criteria and assess competing approaches against these.)

* Do you have your own set of questions ready?

* Do you insist on and assess claims for legitimacy?

* If the issues are beyond your scope, do you call on outside experts before making final decisions?

* Have you practiced saying "NO"?

Take-Away Ideas

* When on the receiving end of communication, activate your critical faculties.

* Look past appearance and into substance.

* Make sure claims are backed up.

* Don't accept glibly—verify.

Part IV

Getting a Good Message

Troilus and Cressida. 3, 2

Now that you have the sender requirements well in hand, it's time to develop the message. The next several chapters will examine what goes into understanding the basis for the message, then organizing it by setting the framework of ideas, and then providing material to support the main points.

Chapter 13

Tuning In: First, Do Your Homework

Beware the ides of March.

Soothsayer, *Julius Caesar*. 1, 2

Before starting that report, heading off to the meeting with thoughts half-collected, or jumping on the computer to start creating bullet charts, take time to do your homework. This is the time to gather information and assess the lay of the land. What's going on? Are there problems? What's the need? Do you have the information pertinent to the issue at hand? This is the G2 or intelligence gathering phase.

Know the Territory

A little touch of Harry in the night.

Chorus, *Henry V, Part II*. 4, 1

Harry, King Henry V, was faced with a big battle against a far superior force. What could he do to head off disaster? His first action was to sound out the troops by applying the management tool known as MBWA (Management by Wandering Around). At night, in disguise, he gathered the sense of the team, found out that morale was weak, and decided to stir up the troops with an all-hands meeting (for that memorable speech, see Chapter 19).

The sales guys in Meredith Willson's *The Music Man* pooh-poohed a competitor because "He doesn't know the territory." Failure to follow that axiom has been the downfall of many. General George Custer thought he was making a smart move until he found himself totally surrounded by Indians at Little Big Horn. Down in Bolivia, Butch Cassidy and the Sundance Kid vastly underestimated the number of soldiers waiting for them before they made their final, fatal dash, at least in the movie.

Watch Out for Information Snags

ARTEMIDORIS Hail Caesar! Read this schedule. . . . Delay not Caesar; read it instantly.

CAESAR What, is the fellow mad?

Julius Caesar. 3, 1

The "schedule" Artemidoris, a teacher of rhetoric, wants desperately to get to Caesar is a note warning him of the upcoming plot to assassinate him. He even names names—including Brutus, Cassius, and others—the same pack who will indeed successfully execute their plot about one page later, with the warning note in Caesar's toga, sliced a bit and never read.

Why would such important information not be given proper attention? Does this ever happen in organizations? A longtime supposition is that advance information that the Japanese forces were moving against Pearl Harbor was sent but either never received, not conveyed to the key people, or not acted upon. As a *sender* of information, it's your responsibility to get it where it needs to be accurately and on time. As a *receiver and decision maker*, it's your responsibility to keep the channels open, to provide an environment that encourages information flow, and to take action.

Organizations often proclaim that they have an open-door policy. Sounds good, and often it may be a good way to keep the information lines open. But, says Keith Davis, in *Human Behavior at Work*, "Though the door physically is open, psychological and social barriers exist which make employees reluctant to enter. *The way the open door can be most effective is for a manager to walk through it and get out among his people.*"

Keep Information Channels Flowing

> The first bringer of unwelcome news
> Hath but a losing office, and his tongue
> Sounds ever after as a sullen bell,
> Remembered tolling a departing friend.
>
> Northumberland, *Henry IV, Part 2*. 1, 1

You'll find that information is easy to acquire when things are going well. However, when things have gone wrong, information is often sparse, as people may be reluctant to convey it. As you are checking the various resources, be careful that your manner doesn't taint the information or cause the flow to dry up.

> They'll have me whipped for speaking true, thou'lt have
> me whipped for lying, and sometimes I am whipped
> for holding my peace.
>
> Fool, *King Lear*. 1, 4

The following account was reported by Geoffrey Brewer:

Xerox Marketing Manager Sam Malone told about a meeting where 3,000 employees gathered in a tent to exchange views with the CEO. When the Q&A segment started, an hourly employee, Frank Enos, stood up to comment about a poorly performing product. To the CEO, David Kearns, he said, "If you had ever bothered to come down and talk to the people who made that product, we could have told you it was no good. And we could have told you why."

Silence. All eyes turned to Enos. Then to Kearns. Then back to Enos.

After what Malone describes as a "prolonged pause," Kearns turned to Enos. As the crowd waited with gut-wrenching anticipation, he said something like, "You're absolutely right. I didn't do that. . . . We will not launch a product again until I have walked the production line."

This moment—call it "Mr. Enos goes to Rochester"—turned out to be one of the most dramatic in Xerox's history. The message Mr. Kearns sent right there was: If you send us bad news, we won't shoot you.

When communication is between different levels, information flow may be affected by either level. Check this dialogue between the *bringer* of the news, Dromio, the slave, and the *receiver*, Adriana, the boss.

DROMIO   So that my errand due unto my tongue,
I thank him, I bare home upon my shoulders;
For, in conclusion, he did beat me there.

ADRIANA   Go back again, thou slave, and fetch him home.

DROMIO   Go back again, and be new beaten home?
For God's sake, send some other messenger
. . . .
If I last in this service you must case me in leather.

Comedy of Errors. 2, 1

At this point Dromio's more than a bit goosy about filling the messenger role. What are the odds that any further information will be objective or complete? What message does this send to other messengers?

A review of your own environment and manner may suggest ways to enhance flow of communication, given that others may be wary of approaching you.

* Check your office. How easy is it for others, especially subordinates, to get into it? Is it a well-protected fortress or an inviting, safe haven?

* Check your room layout. If you want to show you're clearly the boss, make your associates sit on the other side. To help lessen stiffness and hierarchy, have a guest chair beside your desk or move over to a table and chat there.

* Examine the history—yours, your predecessors, and the organization. If others have been living in a world of caution, they'll be cautious.

* Take action to break the barriers in and outside the office. Get out among the troops and chat with them in their turf. Invite a colleague to a business lunch. Check the style of your team meetings. Are they rigidly structured with a strong downward communication process? Some companies have found value in leapfrog meetings, where a supervisor meets with people two levels down. If you're a senior executive, have frequent all-hands meetings, and remember the donuts.

Don't Scorn Too Quickly

SECOND APPARITION   Be bloody, bold, and resolute: laugh to scorn

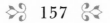 157

The power of man, for none of woman born
Shall harm Macbeth.

MACBETH   Then live, Macduff: what need I fear of thee?

Macbeth. 4, 1

Here the information would prove to be accurate, but it seemed so unlikely, the leader discounted it. This proved to be a serious misjudgment of the meanings; had he considered all the ramifications of the message ("none of woman born"), he might have sought more information and taken early action to wipe out Macduff, the enemy who would do him in (and who was ripped from the womb).

When you get information, check that your receptivity and treatment of it are not polluted by prejudices, inclinations, lack of knowledge, cultural differences, and preconceived perceptions.

I met a fellow employee a few times in the company cafeteria or passing in the halls. She was an hourly employee (clearly evident in those days because the badge said so), had a modest position doing mundane administrative work, and maintained a casual appearance. We typically exchanged chitchat about the weather or gossip—nothing serious because of her modest stature in the company. Later she told me she actually had a Ph.D. and was taking this job to gain experience at the working level. My perception of her had prevented me from truly listening to what she might have been trying to share with me. And she wasn't even an apparition.

San Diego magazine ran a feature article with the cover photograph showing a wild-looking bunch on motorcycles. They had the leather jackets, the slouched hats, boots, beards, hanging keys—a rough-looking crowd you'd likely want to keep at a distance. Inside, the article told about each of the men and women shown on the cover, with another photo showing the group in their professional attire—as the doctors, entrepreneurs, scientists, etc. they actually were. First impressions proved once more to be loaded with misconceptions.

Strolling around the auto museum at one of Nevada's major casinos, I perused the many classic autos on display. I came across an older chap, dressed in a jumpsuit, dusting off the cars. Probably a senior citizen making a few bucks to supplement his modest pension, I thought. We chatted a bit about the cars, and I said that one especially caught my eye. "Really?" he said. "I'm glad you like it, because I own it." Not only that, he owned several of the other cars on display. Gulp. Not exactly the pensioner in need of a few more dollars.

Don't Gloat Too Soon, and Keep Listening

CAESAR   The ides of March are come.

SOOTHSAYER   Ay, Caesar; but not gone.

Julius Caesar. 3, 1

Recall that Caesar had received an earlier warning from the soothsayer. Not only did he give it no credence, but he flouted what he perceived as bad information back at the sender.

Here's another who gives short shrift to input:

> "The purpose you undertake is dangerous."
> —why that's certain: 'tis dangerous to take a cold, to
>   sleep, to drink; but I tell you, my fool lord, out of
>   this nettle, danger, we pluck this flower, safety.
> "The purpose you undertake is dangerous, the friends
>   you have named uncertain, the time itself unsorted,
>   and your whole plot too light, for the counterpoise
>   of so great an opposition."
> Say you so, say you so? I say unto you again, you are a
>   shallow cowardly hind, and you lie. What a lack-
>   brain is this!

Hotspur (reading a warning letter), *Henry IV, Part 1*. 2, 3

Here the boss was given specific details and he still called the sender a fool; other advisors later gave him the same counsel, which he also downplayed. He won the arguments but lost the battle and his life, as the warnings proved accurate.

But that's old-school operation, right? Here are some observations about the communication style of the chairman of a major oil company: "An autocratic ruler with a Napoleon complex who even refused to discuss staff suggestions. . . . Treated exec's disagreement with him as disloyalty. . . . When somebody disagreed with him, he'd eat you alive."

Have you ever made a decision you regretted later? Did you make it on your own, or did you solicit advice from colleagues, specialists, or coaches? If you got advice, did you truly listen to it? Will you make that mistake again? Is this a painful point to be reminded of?

Don't Rush to Judgment

> I know, Iago,
> Thy honesty and love doth mince this matter,
> Making it light to Cassio. Cassio, I love thee;
> But never more be officer of mine.
>
> Othello, *Othello*, 2, 3

Here Othello is firing his trusted deputy, having heard only Iago's report about Cassio assaulting another fellow, when Iago was the culprit behind the whole mess. Big mistake based on poor processing of biased information.

The classic Japanese film *Rashomon* is based on how people perceive a situation very differently based on their backgrounds, information received, and biases.

In my assignment as a corporate ombudsman, employees would

come to me with their unresolved and irritating problems. One lesson I quickly learned was to be sure to get the full story. Often the person with the power to solve the problem had never been informed of the problem. I received a call from an employee who was perturbed because his efforts to get a parking area for motorcycles had gotten nowhere. He was blaming management as nonresponsive. I called the manager in charge of the parking lot and relayed the employee's suggestion. "Really?" he said, "I never heard about that." When a motorcycle space was created a few days later, I called the employee, who was amazed (and delighted) that action was actually taking place.

Getting and Assessing Your "Market"

One of the essential tasks in planning any communication, written or oral, is to understand just who is your target audience. The audience might be one person (interview), a work team (production meeting), a customer (one buyer or a committee), or a large homogeneous group (e.g., the Junior Achievement class for orientation). This applies to almost any interaction, but especially when your success depends on a favorable decision from a senior manager, the buyer for your services, the venture capitalist, or a selection board member.

As a first step, check your network.

* Do you have good channels of information? Are your upward, downward, and cross-communication avenues free-flowing? Have they proven reliable?

* Are you or your colleagues keeping up with the relevant information—that is, market/industry trends, changing environment, personnel issues, and attitudes? Is your information accurate and current? Are you relying too much on one channel?

* Who do you know that knows the people or conditions and what's their take on it?

* How will you get the information you need? Personal phone call, walking the floor, questionnaire, small group brainstorming session?

Second, identify information that is useful to know, such as

* Anything germane to your topic: issues, funding, timing, requirements.

* Who are the key people, the ones with decision making or influencing power?

* How well do they know you, and how well do you know them? Do you and your team have good rapport or bad feelings?

* What do they already know about the topic you will address?

* What are some of their concerns, experiences, and attitudes regarding your topic and proposition? Are you ready to respond to their questions and objections?

* How do they like to receive information, and how do they operate in such meetings? How should you tailor your approach based on that?

* What other options are they likely to consider? What do you know about those? What can you do to head them off?

* What are competitors likely to tell them about you? What can you do about that?

Third, get the info and process it for the basic understanding of your communication.

Take-Away Ideas

* Encourage and seek out communication.

* Process information with an open mind.

* Be careful about discounting input and rushing to conclusions.

* Get the specific information you need and consider this as you plan your approach.

Chapter 14

To Speak and Purpose Not? Set Your Approach

FIRST WITCH   When shall we three meet again
In thunder, lightning or in rain?
SECOND WITCH   When the hurlyburly's done,
When the battle's lost and won.
THIRD WITCH   That will be ere the set of sun.
FIRST WITCH   Where's the place?
SECOND WITCH   Upon the heath.
THIRD WITCH   There to meet with Macbeth.

Macbeth. 1, 1

Now that you've gathered the essential information, what's the plan? The witches are working out the details of their next step, a meeting, clarifying the five Ws: who, what, when, why, where. That's what we'll examine in this chapter: how you take the best information and develop a sound approach and strategy for success.

To Speak and Purpose Not?

It is the purpose that makes strong the vow.

Cassandra, *Troilus and Cressida.* 5, 3

Assuming you've done the useful information gathering described in Chapter 5, a good place to start planning a communication task is to ask "why and what." Why do you want to communicate? What do you expect to achieve?

Whatever communication form you're using, identify clearly the specific objective (one or several) you want to achieve. A task force was meeting regularly to discuss and develop a strategy for effecting change in their organization. One of the problems was that a lot of talk occurred, but action was often difficult. I was brought in as a facilitator for the meetings. In preparation for one of the meetings, the chairman said, "You know what I really like about your approach? You always ask us what we want to achieve." This was not exactly an original concept, but it had been a weakness in their planning.

In coaching and training presentations, I've long stressed the importance of clarifying your objective, the desired outcome. This is often vaguely stated, and it's sometimes difficult for people to state explicitly. The natural question, then, is "How do you know your meeting was successful?"

> I yet beseech your majesty—
> If for I want that glib and oily art,
> To speak and purpose not, since what I well intend
> I'll do't before I speak.
>
> Cordelia, *King Lear*. 1, 1

So what is your objective? Are you hoping to get a larger budget? Do you want a raise? Do you wish to avoid paying the ticket you got for gliding through that stop sign? These fall into the category of persuasion, where you need to convince someone or a group to take action on your proposition. At the close of the session, you will know if you hit your target.

Different types of communication state objectives in different terms from persuasion. The purpose of a status report or procedural change memo is to inform. If you're preparing a roast of the boss for a departmental party, your goal is to entertain. If you want to fire up a new team, your intent is to inspire.

Whatever the type of activity—new employee orientation, asking for a raise, a training session, troubleshooting meeting, bank loan—before you get far into it, write out what you see as your objective.

> That by the help of these, with Him above
> To ratify the work. We may again
> Give to our tables meat, sleep to our nights.
>
> Lord, *Macbeth*. 3, 6

People often have trouble describing explicitly what goal they hope to achieve. So they flounder, strike out in several directions, or drift, lacking a clear target. Personal motivation is affected by whether or not you have a clear goal. Abraham Maslow described well how different needs determine how strongly we are motivated to get involved, decide to take action, or become passionate about a cause.

Financial reward, even good old greed, can be a strong motivator. Here's a tip: write down exactly what you want to achieve in financial terms, and see if that doesn't help focus your attention.

Right Wavelength?

> I heard thee speak me a speech once, but it was never
>   acted; or if it was, not above once; for the play, I
>   remember, pleas'd not the million; 'twas caviar to the
>   general.
>
> Hamlet (to the players), *Hamlet*. 2, 2

When shaping your plan, have you taken into account the backgrounds and interests of those with whom you will communicate (that good information you pursued in Chapter 13)? This may seem obvious but often isn't.

At my company, we had regular meetings with the senior executive team to discuss plans and progress. To improve communication, management decided to pass this same information on to the entire supervisory work team. This was welcomed by the supervisors. It proved to be a total flop, as the material presented was at a level that top managers could understand, but was nearly incomprehensible to the first and second levels of supervisors. Good information, wrong audience.

About that caviar . . . I had scheduled a meeting out on the factory floor, with the purpose of recognizing several machinists for their long service. It was a mixed group of machinists and senior management, with the vice president giving a brief talk. I thought some coffee and donuts might get people mixing and reduce the hierarchical barriers. Good in concept, but bad in execution, as the refreshments arrived very late. We had to proceed with the ceremony, and the environment was stiff. Finally the refreshments arrived, and the hobnobbing and war stories ensued. The donuts were the key; caviar wouldn't have done the job.

> Prithee, be silent, boy; I profit not by thy talk.
>
> Thersites, *Troilus and Cressida*. 5, 1

How often do we find ourselves sitting in a meeting and wishing we were elsewhere, because the topic under discussion is of low interest to us? As the one attempting to communicate, you need to find out pertinent information about the receivers, those you're trying to reach.

The information you have about your listeners is key to knowing how to formulate your message to them. If you underestimate their knowledge, you may end up talking down to them; if you over-estimate it, you can find yourself talking over their heads, leaving them baffled.

No Respect Begets No Respect

BRUTUS   We pray the gods he may deserve your loves.

SECOND CITIZEN   Amen sir: to my poor unworthy notice,
He mock'd us when he begg'd our voices.

THIRD CITIZEN   Certainly
He flouted us downright.
. . . .
He's not confirm'd; we may deny him yet.

SECOND CITIZEN   And will deny him:
I'll have five hundred voices of that sound.

Coriolanus. 2, 3

You may find yourself making an even greater mistake with your audiences by not respecting them or patronizing them. Before the previous exchange, Coriolanus had made that mistake when he was obligated to go before the citizens to ask their approval of him as consul. He did this grudgingly, went in with a bad attitude, and came across as being above the rabble. They did approve him—after all, he was a war hero—but his enemies aimed to reverse that vote. They were successful because Coriolanus had talked down to the citizens before, and they resented it. Belittle employees and they'll find ways to get back at you.

Critical Point: The Plan

ANTONY That's all I seek:
And am moreover suitor that I may
Produce his body to the market-place,
And, in the pulpit, as becomes a friend,
Speak in the order of his funeral.

BRUTUS You shall, Mark Antony.

CASSIUS Brutus, a word with you.
(Aside to Brutus) You know not what you do: do not
    consent
That Antony speak in his funeral.

Julius Caesar. 3, 1

You probably know the line "Friends, Romans, Countrymen." That almost didn't happen. Here Antony makes a request to speak at the funeral of Caesar, whom Brutus and team have just wiped out. Cassius—he of the lean and hungry look—is advising strongly against letting that happen (he has a larger view of the situation), but Brutus agrees to Antony's request. This sets the stage for arguably the most famous speech in Shakespeare, which completely undoes the Brutus-Cassius team. Major strategic error.

Based on all your information, you've now focused your goal and targeted your audience. Are you making the right decisions as you continue to shape your plan? It's good to review this before proceeding, as this sets the basis for everything else. Guess right, no problem. Guess wrong and head down the wrong path, and you will be expending resources toward a bad effort.

A good idea at this point is to solicit guidance from a review team, third party (as devil's advocate), or colleague. Being less entwined in the details, they can bring an objective viewpoint, or even ask some "dumb" questions that can redirect your plan. That is especially valuable while it's still early in the process—valuable, that is, if you listen to what they say, as opposed to giving them short shrift, as Brutus did.

Let's continue a bit further along in this saga and see where ignoring good advice trips up another top manager. This is the same Antony who was so successful just before.

Ignore Market Warnings, at Your Peril

ANTONY   Canidus, we fight with him by sea. (*and that's that!*)

. . . .

CANIDUS   But these offers,
Which serve not for his vantage, he shakes off;
And so should you.

ENOBARBUS   Your ships are not well mann'd.
Your mariners are muleters, reapers, people
Ingrossed by swift impress.

. . . .

ANTONY   By sea, by sea. (*What do you know, Eno?*)

ENOBARBUS   Most worthy sir, you therein throw away
The absolute soldiership you have by land. . . .

ANTONY   I'll fight at sea. (*My heels are dug in.*)

. . . .

SOLDIER   O noble emperor, do not fight by sea;
Trust not to rotten planks . . .

We have used to conquer standing on the earth
And fighting foot to foot. (*You're giving up our strengths,
you nincompoop . . . sir.*)

ANTONY   Well, well; away! (*Get lost, punk! You're not even
an officer!*)

SOLDIER   By Hercules, I think I am i' the right. (*And he
was.*)

Antony and Cleopatra. 3, 7 (Comments added)

Keep your sensing antenna on alert, and stay flexible if information
surfaces that contradicts earlier strategy decisions. Perhaps Antony
got cocky after he outwitted the Brutus team and was permitted to
make that great speech. Perhaps his intuitive instincts, so well honed
before, have gone into slumber mode; after all, he's been partying a
lot with Cleopatra by now. At any rate, he ignored advice from a
variety of intelligent folks, from the highest rank to the foot soldier—
they all knew he was making a mistake—and got whipped badly.

Major corporate decisions have been documented that went in
the face of what the G2 seemed to indicate. Remember when Coca-
Cola phased out their tried and tested product for the New Coke?
It turned out that a huge contingent of their market really liked the
old Coke. Give them credit: they brought back the original product
to pair with the new Coke.

During the 2000 Olympics a Nike ad, in a very expensive slot,
showed a young woman grooming herself in a mirror in her own
bedroom, when a masked intruder suddenly appeared with a chain-
saw. She was terrified and fled screaming, the intruder in hot pursuit.
She raced through the woods and fell, he was almost on her, and
finally she outran him. The point, apparently, was if you stay in
shape, you'll be able to get away when attacked. This ad totally
backfired, as NBC's phone lines and the Internet Web sites were
besieged with protests from outraged viewers. Were the blinders on
when this ad went through the planning and screening process?

Where was a Cassius, Enobarbus, or even a foot soldier? What am I missing?

Fifteen years ago I walked into my first wholesale warehouse, a short distance from my office, and said, "Wow! This is one booming business." First-hand information. Also about that time I became aware of a start-up telecommunications company, headed by an entrepreneur I knew had great success with his previous company and said, "This is bound to be a big success!" Did I buy any stock in Price Club, later acquired by Costco, or Qualcomm? Of course not. Which is why this is a book on communication, not investing.

Dare I mention the Edsel?

Got a Plan? Money to Make It Happen?

> . . . whose large style
> Agrees not with the leanness of his purse.
>
> Gloucester, Henry VI, Part 2. 1, 1

> I wasted time, and now doth time waste me.
>
> Richard (about to be executed) Richard II. 5, 5

The clock is ticking. Good intentions need to be backed with a sound approach. Many people are afflicted with procrastination, and they delay until they either drop the whole idea or scramble like mad to catch up. Have you ever found yourself facing an 8 A.M. meeting deadline, and realize about 5 P.M. the day before that you're a long way from ready? Found yourself setting the alarm for 4 A.M. so you can jolt yourself awake to put the final details on that report? Found yourself on the plane heading for Boston, working feverishly on the laptop to somehow come up with a presentation that won't embarrass you too much? Then you're among that large pack who could benefit from better time management.

What's here? the portrait of a blinking idiot,
Presenting me with a schedule! I will read it.

Prince Arragon, *The Merchant of Venice.* 2, 9

Now that you've assessed the basics of your communication task, this is a good point to lay out the schedule for getting it done. This may be as simple as marking a few milestones on your Day-Timer or calendar program. Putting them in writing ups the chances that those key actions will actually occur. For a more complex task, use a good project management program or scheduling tool, such as a Gantt chart.

Here are some tips to suit your deadlines and wallet, and avoid those last-minute panics:

* List the main tasks to get the job done.

* Set the key milestones for a sensible progression.

* Communicate the plan to any contributors. Get their buy-in.

* *Keep tracking the plan* and the outlays to make sure all is on course and within budget.

* Act fast if slips or overruns occur, to get back on target.

O, call back yesterday, bid time return.

Salisbury, *Richard II.* 3, 2

Take-Away Ideas

* Set a clear goal.

* Weigh all the key factors in developing your approach.

* Give serious attention to feedback from advisors.

* Put a workable plan in place, and get moving.

Chapter 15

Bait the Hook Well:
Organize Your Material

They have committed false report; moreover, they have
   spoken untruths; secondarily, they are slanders; sixth
   and lastly, they have belied a lady; thirdly, they have
   verified unjust things; and to conclude, they are lying
   knaves.

Dogberry, *Much Ado About Nothing*. 5, 1

The next step in preparing for your upcoming communication is to
organize your topics in a workable order: outline, meeting agenda,
training plan, storyboard for a presentation or video, checklist for a
phone chat. How can you get their attention, hold it through the
main points, and then wind up with a successful conclusion?

Sort Out Your Information

All the world's a stage,
And all the men and women merely players:
They have their exits and their entrances;

And one man in his time plays many parts,
His acts being seven ages. At first the infant,
Mewling and puking in the nurses arms.
Then the whining school-boy. . . .
And then the lover, sighing like furnace. . . .
Then a soldier, full of strange oaths. . . .
And then the justice, in fair round belly. . . .
The sixth age shifts into the lean and slipper'd
   pantaloon. . . .
Last scene of all,
That ends this strange eventful history,
Is second childishness and mere oblivion,
Sans teeth, sans eyes, sans taste, sans everything.

Jaques, *As You Like It*. 2, 7

It's easy to talk about a topic if you have no concerns about time, audience interest, or clarity. Just ramble away. That mode of communication may work for casual conversation, up to the point where your listener falls asleep or excuses herself for something more important.

In many business situations, that approach doesn't work well. You will have a time or page limit to convey your information; the receivers will expect organized and focused material; and if they have difficulty following your story, they'll likely interrupt your spoken message—"Get to the point"—or dispose of your written ones in the circular file cabinet beside the desk. As this is not the outcome you probably desire, taking time to organize your material is a wise investment.

Fit Your Message to the Rules

The time is out of joint.

Hamlet, *Hamlet*. 1, 5

Make sure you know the guidelines set for your report, presentation, phone call, or one-on-one meeting with the boss. What you can cover has to fit within the page or time limit. Then, within that limit, you can allocate time for each of the major elements.

At a national convention, I was in the audience for a session on leadership. The speaker may have had a good program, had this been a three-hour meeting instead of one-hour. His format included way too many items, with several time-consuming group activities. His time budget was not workable, so the session ended up a total waste.

> Make use of time, let not advantage slip.
>
> *Venus and Adonis.* 129

Does this sound familiar? A meeting has been called to review a number of options and decide on a specific plan. The meeting will last one hour only, because another group has the conference room scheduled. The meeting starts late, several people straggle in, and reading of the minutes takes up the first ten minutes. A new procedure has to be explained and argued over. Then comes a discussion about who will bring what for the department picnic.

Finally, discussion of the main issue starts, with a short presentation of the first of six options. A lengthy discussion ensues. Then the second option is presented, but the presentation goes way over the allotted time. It's almost time to end the meeting, so options 3–6 get about one minute each. Then the vote is called for, with everybody groaning that they didn't have time to digest and discuss all the options. So the decision is tabled for another meeting.

So what went wrong? A poor meeting plan, a poor meeting manager, poor attendees, and lack of agenda or discipline. Result: another wasted meeting, with no results.

The degree of firmness to the rules can vary greatly. For written proposals, the specs may be absolute, such as 100 pages total, with page limits for each required topic. Reports and memos generally aren't that strict, yet it's still good to find out what is considered acceptable. Know the style of the principal receiver: some insist on one page, others want the full treatment. One manager made it clear he wanted material in graphic and visual form, not pages of written information. Another ignored a two-inch-thick report, with the comment that he had no interest or time to wade through all that. Bad audience analysis.

> Good business must be wrought ere noon.
>
> Hecate, *Macbeth*. 3, 5

For personal communication, such as meetings, presentations, or training sessions, pay attention to the limitations of the human body. Consider what will happen if you schedule a dry, fact-laden, slide-illustrated presentation right after lunch, with the lights dimmed. Can you schedule that topic for the morning, with a detailed Q&A session, a plant tour, or the highly involving "ropes course" after lunch? Maybe not.

Got a Hook?

> Bait the hook well; this fish will bite.
>
> Claudio, *Much Ado About Nothing*. 2, 3

As a meeting or conference starts, many attendees are still thinking about what a delicious bagel they had, and what time they must slip away to check their messages. If you're running the meeting or you're the opening speaker, your first task is to get the audience on board. If you're submitting a report, how can you get the boss or customer to start reading it?

Develop a hook, an attention-getting opener, appropriate to the type of communication.

* The writer of an important memo put at the top of page one a highlighted crisp summary of the degree of the problem and what the report would resolve. In 20 seconds the reader would conclude this was worthwhile reading. A good quote can also serve to catch the attention, such as one from William Shakespeare (find your own).

* An imaginative facilitator for a community planning meeting started by noting that several priorities had to be considered. He started juggling a tennis ball, symbolizing recreation, added an acorn, for the environment, and then a wrench, for development. With him juggling three items, we were on board, plus we were aware of the need to listen to other viewpoints.

* For a safety meeting the leader asked everybody to close their eyes and visualize the most delightful scene they knew— perhaps the kids playing in the park, a sunset at the beach, or a flower in full bloom. "Suppose," he said, "that for the rest of your life, this is the only way you could see this scene." From here, with the audience on board, he moved into the topic of discussion: the need to wear safety glasses.

> Romans, countrymen and lovers! hear me for my cause, and be silent, that you may hear.
>
> Brutus, *Julius Caesar*. 3, 2

What's your reaction to this opening? "Shut the hell up and pay attention!" With some audiences, even a vice president or two, I've often thought this is what I'd like to say, but it somehow never seemed wise. A bit on the arrogant side.

> Friends, Romans, Countrymen, lend me your ears;
> I come to bury Caesar, not to praise him.
>
> Marc Antony, *Julius Caesar*. 3, 2

This opening occurred about ten minutes after the previous one. This started that speech Brutus was strongly warned against allowing. With this opening everybody knew right away what this talk was going to cover (except Antony was lying, sneaky devil). This opening has been duplicated only about 800 million times over the past four centuries.

Having the attention of your audience is only one of the activities that are important in the opening of the meeting. To ensure a productive meeting, it is often wise to have an advance meeting with key players, communicate key information to attendees, and make sure the donuts will be on hand. Then at the start of the meeting.

* Identify yourself and your credentials.
* Do a quick fill-in of previous meetings or events.
* Clarify session objectives, often with group input.
* Address the session format or agenda, with time budgets.
* Clarify roles of active meeting personnel.
* Get buy-in from attendees.

Now Help Them Get It

PORTER   Faith, sir, we were carousing till the second cock: and drink, sir, is a great provoker of three things.

MACDUFF   What three things does drink especially
provoke?

PORTER   Marry, sir, nose-painting, sleep, and urine.
Lechery, sir, it provokes and unprovokes; it provokes
the desire, but it takes away the performance: therefore
much drink may be said to be an equivocator with
lechery: it makes him and it mars him; it sets him on
and it takes him off; it persuades him and disheartens
him; makes him stand to and not stand to; in
conclusion, equivocates him in a sleep, and giving him
the lie, leaves him.

Macbeth. 2, 3

For the main part of your communication, sequence your messages
so they will (1) be easily followed, (2) focus essential information,
(3) make a convincing argument, (4) meet time constraints, and (5)
achieve your objectives.

Several tools can be helpful in developing an effective layout for
your communication:

* *Mindmapping* is a cousin to doodling. On a piece of paper
  or chalkboard, you let the ideas flow and develop into a
  linked relationship of main and secondary ideas.

* *Brainstorming* helps get ideas surfaced, and then sorted with
  3 × 5 cards or Post-Its on a board or folder.

* *Outlining* is easily done using software packages, and then
  fleshed out with details or visuals.

* *Storyboarding* combines your outline with visual concepts,
  and can be done with pages on the wall or with the
  computer screen using presentation software.

Here are some options for structuring a report or presentation:

* A simple numbered set (Letterman's Top 10 lists, Covey's Seven Habits)

* Time sequence (past, present, future)

* Steps in a process (design, build, deliver, sell)

* Cause-and-effect relationship (problem-solution)

* Parts of the product (engine, frame, body, . . .)

* Report by organization (safety, finance, engineering)

* Coding (four Ps of Presentations; ABCD for melanoma self-check—Asymmetrical shape, Border irregular, Color not consistent, Diameter larger than a pencil)

* Repeated theme (the politicos' favorite: "I have a dream . . .")

For other communication types, tailor your format to fit specific objectives, styles, urgency, audience size, and so on. Some examples:

* Meeting, primarily reporting (update, reports by topic, discussion, directions, action items)

* Meeting, interaction, e.g., problem solving session (brainstorm, discuss, evaluate, select)

* Training session (state objectives, explain, illustrate, try out, test, clarify)

Check Your Logic

In manner and form following, sir; all those three.

Costard, *Love's Labour's Lost.* 1, 1

JULIET   Not proud you have, but thankful that you have:
Proud can I never be of what I hate;
But thankful even for hate that is meant love.

HER FATHER   How, how! how, how! chop-logic? What is
this?

Romeo and Juliet. 3, 5

If you present an argument that won't stand up under logical analysis, you're not likely to have success. The training associated with most business disciplines stresses clarity, relationships, critical thinking, and logical arguments. So if you have holes in your argument, or are trying the flim-flam route of persuasion, watch out.

In spite of that discipline, many finished reports and presentations reveal flaws when subjected to the scrutiny of logic and legitimacy. One of the best ways to spot holes is with a bare-bones outline, where the main and subsidiary points aren't loaded up with content. Reviewing material while it's still in the early stages of development has helped many people tighten up their clarity.

Be Alert for Information Overload

FOOL   Sirrah, I'll teach thee a speech.

LEAR   Do.

FOOL   Mark it, nuncle:
Have more than thou showest,
Speak less that thou knowest.

King Lear 1, 4

How often do we attempt to tell everything we know about the subject to our readers and listeners, who soon go into the MEGO (my eyes glaze over) mode?

This is too long.

Polonius, *Hamlet.* 2, 2

The project manager (PM) arrived to give an update to the vice president. He placed a large stack of transparencies on the table next to the overhead projector, started talking, showed only the top six visuals, and ended the presentation. The VP was surprised at the conciseness of the report, and asked what all those other transparencies were for. The PM said those were extras, in case of questions. The VP said, "I was so concerned about the large number of transparencies, I didn't pay any attention to what you were saying." The PM's lesson learned was to keep standby visuals hidden so that listeners pay better attention.

If you've done good audience assessment, you're less likely to overburden the receiver in your written reports or presentations. But you don't always have full information, so you need to be tuned in to what the receiver is willing to accept. If you plan in flexibility with your material, you can shift gears as warranted to still get across the key information and achieve your objectives. Some tips:

* Have a concise executive summary of your material, either written or presented.

* Be prepared with two or three levels of material (e.g., in a presentation if the receiver says five minutes, you've got it; if he says twenty, you've got it).

* Trim the basic package to the essential points, and include a substantial dialogue segment for whatever details the receiver wants to pursue. Have extra "just-in-case" materials on hand, such as backup visual aids or details of trade studies or test results. The receiver may not care, but you can make the best of your time slot if you're prepared.

Be Able to Summarize

> Give me your hand. I can tell your fortune. You are a
> fool.
>
> Daughter, *The Two Noble Kinsmen.* 3, 5

Now that was indeed a concise summary. For presentations, this is known as the elevator speech. This is what you say when you arrive at the sixth floor ready to brief the vice president, who says, "Got to catch a plane. Hop on the elevator and tell me your story." You have from the sixth to the ground floor to state your case. Do this as well with your written reports or telephone discussions.

Being able to summarize is of high importance in communication. I've heard senior management in many industries remark how much they value the concise summary. Venture capitalists typically want to know in the first few minutes the essence of your story. The up-front or executive summary is often stated in written or spoken form in reports and briefings.

Former British Prime Minister John Major, recalled a conversation with the Russian president. "I asked Boris Yeltsin to tell me briefly what the situation in Russia was like. 'Good,' he said. I asked him for the longer version, in two words. 'Not good,' he said."

Get Closure, Commitment, and Action!

> There must be conclusions.
>
> Nym, *Henry V.* 2, 1

As you wrap up your communication, several activities are useful. Whatever the communication vehicle—meeting, presentation, or training session—it's especially important to concisely summarize the content: the main points that were made, the new understandings that have been reached, and the specific agreements made. Delineate all actions that have been committed to, the person responsible, and deadlines.

PORTIA   Good sentences, and well pronounced.

NERISSA   They would be better, if well followed.

The Merchant of Venice. 1, 2

What you don't want is the comment that it sure read or sounded fine, with the action amounting to nothing. That can occur for many reasons: weak arguments, not addressing a critical concern, inadequate urgency focus, overtaken by other events. If your purpose is to achieve a specific action on the part of the audience, clearly ask for the order.

BENEDICK   Come, bid me do any thing for thee.

BEATRICE   Kill Claudio.

Much Ado About Nothing. 4, 1

Finally, if the communication calls for a send-off message, such as a team-building event, give them a punchy closer that will leave them with a reinforcing message and a zest for making it happen. This is the coach's half-time speech to rally the troops.

And once again bestride our foaming steeds,
And once again cry, "Charge upon our foes!"
But never once again turn back and fly.

Warwick, *Henry VI, Part 3.* 2, 1

Take-Away Ideas

* Take time to organize your ideas.
* Meet the requirements whatever the format.
* Make your messages clear, concise, and convincing.
* Hook 'em, enlighten 'em, move 'em out.
* Build in flexibility.

Chapter 16

Let Us Tell Sad Stories:
Develop the Substance

And if thou tell'st the heavy story right,
Upon my soul, the hearers will shed tears.

Duke of York, *Henry VI, Part 3*. 1, 4

There is power in communication. If done well, it can bring about change, convince juries, and mobilize an army. But how is that accomplished? In the last chapter we saw how effective organization of your message can add to its power. Having laid out the structure, you need to give listeners solid substance that will help them understand, stay tuned, believe, and be inspired. You have plenty of options at your disposal.

Where's the Beef?

It is a tale
Told by an idiot, full of sound and fury,
Signifying nothing.

Macbeth, *Macbeth*. 5, 5

Without solid substance, your communication may well be regarded as fluffy and perhaps entertaining but of little value. You've undoubtedly experienced communication of this sort from a variety of venues. A political speaker heavy on the sound and fury but light on specifics. A preacher with lots of fire and little take-away.

Here's a quick test. One hour after you've heard a program, try to recall the main points or perhaps one or two lessons learned. The program's intention may have been purely to entertain—a noble purpose—but most business communications have specific messages and changes in mind.

> I have heard
> That guilty creatures, sitting at a play,
> Have by the very cunning of the scene
> Been struck so to the soul that presently
> They have proclaim'd their malefactions;
> For murder, though it have no tongue, will speak
> With most miraculous organ.
>
> Hamlet, *Hamlet.* 2, 2

Whether listening to persuasive trial lawyers, politicians, or program corporate marketeers, audiences can be won over with a sound argument, or lost with a weak one. The support or evidence you use is a key element in achieving your communication goal.

> ANTONY   You all did see that on the Lupercal
> I thrice presented him a kingly crown,
> Which he did thrice refuse; was this ambition?
> Yet Brutus says he was ambitious,
> And sure, he is an honorable man.
> I speak not to disprove what Brutus spoke,
> But here I am to speak what I do know . . .

FIRST CITIZEN   Methinks there is much reason in his
   sayings.

Julius Caesar. 3, 2

If you intend to bring about increased awareness, enhanced knowledge, or a changed attitude, good support or substantiation for your
cause is key. *State the point* you want to make (e.g., speaking to your
work team, "we need to upgrade our computer graphics capability"),
and then, to make the case, *state "for example,"* and provide some
supporting information, such as

* A case history or anecdote relating the many problems that
  occurred on the last major effort because of poor systems

* Productivity statistics of new systems versus the present
  antiquated one

* Specific examples of what competitors X and Y are now
  using and their success

* Testimonials from other users about what great results they've
  had

* Comparing receivers' frequent (and expensive) investment in
  the latest Big Bertha golf club with the similar value of
  investing in an upgraded computer system

* A quote from a credible source that gets people thinking it's
  time to act

A Story, Sad or Happy, Often Works

For God's sake, let us sit upon the ground
And tell sad stories of the death of kings.

Richard, *Richard II. 3, 2*

Once you have determined the message to impart, how you choose to reinforce that message is the next important piece. Telling a story, providing strong evidence, or citing testimony from credible sources can be powerful in winning over an audience. Famed attorney Gerry Spence, in his book *How To Argue and Win Every Time*, says the heart of successful persuasion is to tell them a story. "Storytelling is in the genes. Listening to stories is also in the genes. It follows, therefore, that the most effective structure for any argument will always be *story*."

HERMIONE   What wisdom stirs amongst you? Come, sir, now
I am for you again; pray you, sit by us,
And tell 's a tale.

MAMILLIUS   Merry or sad shall't be?

HERMIONE   As merry as you will.

MAMILLIUS   A sad tale's best for winter: I have one
Of sprites and goblins.

HERMIONE   Let's have that, good sir.
Come on, sit down: come on, and do your best
To fright me with your sprites. You're powerful at it.

The Winter's Tale. 2, 1

Master communicators almost always tell stories well. In his book *In Search of Excellence* and on the lecture circuit, Tom Peters masterfully applies stories in the form of case histories, success stories, or miscues from organizations, techniques they've used, results attained, or effects on the work team. On National Public Radio's *Prairie Home Companion*, Garrison Keillor has been holding his audiences for years with his tales about life in the mythical Midwestern town of Lake Wobegon.

Yet, by your gracious patience,
I will a round unvarnish'd tale deliver
Of my whole course of love
. . . .
Wherein I spake of most disastrous chances,
Of moving accidents by flood and field,
Of hair-breadth 'scapes i' the imminent deadly breach,
Of being taken by the insolent foe,
And sold to slavery, of my redemption thence . . .
My story being done,
She gave me for my pains a world of sighs.

Othello, Othello. 1, 3

A good story can thus achieve good rewards, as Othello describes Desdemona's reaction upon hearing his tale. The next step was marriage, intrigue, and eventual disaster, but that's another story.

Suppose you're going before the city council to urge them to put a stop sign at a busy corner. Do you have a good story to tell them, such as about the speeding car that hit two third-graders on their way to school? That one story, well stated, may do the job.

In a safety meeting, your job is to get the other members to go back to their departments and implement the new stricter policy on wearing helmets in construction areas. The workers know they're supposed to do that, but they've gotten lax. Maybe an effective motivator is the story of their colleague, Gale, who got clobbered by a falling wrench while not wearing his helmet. Describe Gale's ride in the ambulance, the painful four-hour operation, and slow recovery program to restore normal speech.

Paint Pictures (of Imaginary Puissance?)

And let us, ciphers to this great accompt,
On your imaginary forces work.

Suppose within the girdle of these walls
Are now confined two mighty monarchies,
Whose high-upreared and abutting fronts
The perilous narrow ocean parts asunder:
Piece out the imperfections with your thoughts;
Into a thousand parts divide one man,
And make imaginary puissance;
Think, when we talk of horses, that you see them
Printing their proud hoofs i' the receiving earth;
For 'tis your thoughts that now must deck our kings.

Henry V. Prologue.

One proven way to hold and convince an audience is to verbally paint a picture for them. Shakespeare's narrator did just that by describing the bare stage and only a few actors so that listeners used their own senses to give the scenes realism.

Recall the power of radio drama, where the story unfolds entirely in the minds of the listeners. I recall as a youth vividly seeing mysterious and spooky creatures that would stay with me for days. With the help of sound effects, I could see that Inner Sanctum door creaking open, and Jack Benny winding his way past various traps to his legendary vault.

In the written and spoken word, some masters of picturesque language have been Carl Sandburg, Robert Frost, and Maya Angelou.

In the political arena, adept at describing reality as she wanted voters to see it was Texas Governor Ann Richards. She laced her 1988 Democratic Convention keynote speech with colorful descriptions of her side's successes and the other side's failures, using picturesque phraseology—"that hound won't hunt!"—for humor and effect. (On the other hand this picturesque stuff may be overrated—her candidate, Michael Dukakis, lost to a chap named Bush, and then she lost her own next election to a younger chap named Bush.)

Make Support Vivid

> I think the King is but a man, as I am: the violet smells
> to him as it doth to me; the element shows to him as
> it doth to me; all his senses have but human
> conditions; his ceremonies laid by, in his nakedness
> he appears but a man.
>
> King Henry, *Henry V.* 4, 1

This is actually the King in disguise, speaking of himself to the camped troops. Perhaps this phraseology will sound familiar to one-time high school athletes. To calm the fears of their charges about the tough opponents they were about to face, coaches were known for proclaiming, "Remember, they put on their pants one leg at a time, just as you do." Somehow it never seemed convincing when I was a 120-pound marginal quarterback and the players on the opposing line averaged 235 pounds.

In 1993 GTE had just gone through many changes, so their 1993 strategy meeting with senior officers was directed by the president to reflect the changing world and the need for new ways of thinking. Mary Beth Bardin, vice president of public affairs, described some approaches they used for the meeting. To focus on teamwork, they invited three Air Force Thunderbird pilots, who told about how trust among a team of pilots can mean life or death in combat. When Chrysler built the new Viper sports car, it was critical that all involved work together. They brought in champion dog racer Susan Butcher, whose dog teams have won several of the grueling Alaska Iditarod races. She told how teamwork and trust between her and the dogs led to survival and victory.

So when you need to add spice to your next meeting, broaden your thinking (and budget).

Make 'em Laugh

If you desire the spleen, and will laugh yourself into
stitches, follow me.

Maria, *Twelfth Night*. 3, 2

Humor has a special power in much business communication. In tense situations, it can break the air of hostility. In meetings it can set a tone of camaraderie. In presentations it can provide an appreciated change of pace from facts and litanies, regain attention, and perhaps make the case better than sober methods can.

At a meeting intended to get people working together better, the facilitator had teams craft makeshift gadgets and then use these to catch eggs tossed by teammates. This was great entertainment, as the teams kept moving further and further apart until, splat, their eggs went onto the tarp the leader had wisely provided. They were having fun while learning the value of teamwork.

In office cubicles, meetings, and presentations, *Dilbert* or *Far Side* cartoons are staples for getting laughs while making a point about bosses (a common target), meetings (mostly useless), and colleagues (mostly weird). Probably the main staple of e-mails that make the rounds of corporate computers are jokes, some of them even funny.

During the 2000 presidential campaign, Democratic vice presidential candidate Joe Lieberman displayed a good knack for telling stories. With one audience he expressed some concern about the joke he was about to tell because it had some mildly coarse language. He told of a kid who was having trouble because the wheels kept falling off his wagon. In exasperation, he said, "Well I'll be damned!" A minister heard him and said, "Son, that's not good. You should say 'Praise the Lord!' " When the kid's wheels fell off again, he said

"Praise the Lord!," whereupon the wheels flew right back onto the wagon. The preacher saw this and said, "Well I'll be damned!"

Make 'em Weep

> I come no more to make you laugh: things now,
> That bear a weighty and a serious brow,
> Sad, high and working, full of state and woe,
> Such noble scenes as draw the eye to flow,
> We now present. Those that can pity, here
> May, if they think it well, let fall a tear.
>
> Prologue, *Henry VIII*.

Would you expect hilarity in a story of a man who phases out eight wives, several by beheading? These words have a special place for true fans of the Bard, as this was his final work.

Using real examples of people in difficulty has proven effective in the company appeal for support of the charitable campaign. Adding power is telling how the company's generous contributions have helped a child get facial reconstruction.

Political conventions are especially good for weaving in stories of people who have overcome severe hardships, and you can count on one or two of them being called out from their seats in high-visibility locations. Sally Struthers and Rob Reiner played the young married couple who for years made us laugh on the TV show *All in the Family*. They've both become effective at making us weep, and reach for the checkbook, with their heartfelt tales dramatizing their respective causes. And almost any program with Tammy Faye Baker was guaranteed to produce some tears, hers if not the audience's.

Tap into a Hot Button

But here's a parchment with the seal of Caesar;
I found it in his closet; 'tis his will:
But let the commons hear this testament—
Which pardon me, I do not mean to read—
And they would go and kiss dead Caesar's wounds.

Mark Antony, *Julius Caesar.* 3, 2

A primary path to successful persuasion is to address a key need of listeners—a "hot button"—and show how they will benefit from your proposed course of action. To be most effective, the support material you use should tap into the concerns and interests of your audience. Pick examples that listeners can readily relate to, respond to, and maybe benefit from.

Antony found a good one—the will in which Caesar left his goods to the people. Here, as in many cases, money in their pockets is the hot button that will move them toward Antony's true objective. Greed usually works, but not always. And darn if they didn't insist that Antony, despite his vigorous protestation, do indeed read that will.

ALL   The will, the will! We will hear Caesar's will . . .

ANTONY   If you have tears, prepare to shed them now . . .
O, now you weep, and I perceive you feel
The dint of pity: these are gracious drops.
Kind souls, what weep you when you but behold
Our Caesar's vesture wounded? Look you here—
Here is himself, marr'd as you see, with traitors.

CITIZENS (VARIOUS)   O piteous spectacle! O noble
  Caesar! O woeful day! O traitors, villains!

ALL   Revenge! About! Seek! Burn! Fire! Kill! Slay! Let not a
       traitor live!

Julius Caesar. 3, 2

Think you can get this kind of results with your own tale of woe,
and a good hot button?

Make Their Hair Stand on End

I could a tale unfold whose lightest word
Would harrow up thy soul, freeze thy young blood,
Make thy two eyes, like stars, start from their spheres,
Thy knotted and combined locks to part,
And each particular hair to stand on end
Like quills upon the fearful porpentine [porcupine].

Ghost of Hamlet's father, *Hamlet.* 1, 5

A good spooky story is the staple of kids' campfires. Remember a
scary movie, and the effect the especially horrible scenes left on you?
How about Alfred Hitchcock's *Psycho*, where one scene led many
people to be afraid to step in the shower for months? Or Peter
Benchley's *Jaws*, which kept people out of the ocean for a decade?
On a recent flight, I went through an orange cloud coming up from
a fire below. Spooky. My seat mate said he expected to see a little
man appear out on the wing, a memorable scene from Rod Serling's
Twilight Zone. Who doesn't remember these shows?

About those unsafe work practices in the workplace: Would a
projected slide showing a banged up eye get people thinking about
those safety glasses? It might resonate with some people, but not
with others.

Nothing like a good jolt of realism to catch people's attention.
A much-discussed antismoking ad features a woman speaking from

an electronic voice box because throat cancer has wiped out her vocal cords. That itself made the ad powerful, but it became unforgettable when the woman lifted a cigarette to the hole in her throat and drew in another puff.

That tale jolted a lot of nonsmokers, but did it change behavior? If you're conducting a stop-smoking class, it helps to have a variety of examples, as one person might not be affected by example A but might by example B (Maslow's hierarchy of needs). Perhaps another example would reach at least one or two more. This was the true story about Sonny Barger, a name synonymous with the wildest days of the Hells' Angels during the 1960s and 1970s. You could compare photos, of the old Barger, shouting and cursing (and smoking heavily), with the Barger of today speaking in a much muted tone, through a voice box, as he also has lost his vocal cords. Would this get someone's attention? Motivate him or her to change behavior.

Still no reaction? Don't give up. Try the Motley Fool's calculation: Instead of smoking one pack of day, you take that money and diligently invest it. If you start that at age 35, when you're ready to retire at 65, applying 11 percent per year gain, you'll be worth another $241,900. Works for me.

Do Your Stories Lose Audiences?

> Their copious stories, oftentimes begun,
> End without audience, and are never done.
>
> *Venus and Adonis*

We've seen that having a story to tell can be valuable; yet, if not used well, that story may be detrimental to your communication. Hal Holbrook as Mark Twain tells a story and keeps adding side tales as he goes. Unfortunately, he rambles so much that the point is lost, and so is the audience. Finally, Twain goes to sleep himself, still mumbling the never-ending tale.

We tend to appreciate a person who can tell a good story or joke, but if that person adds another story, and then another, we look for the "gong" bell or exit. Some of us are not great storytellers. Did you ever start a joke and get confused partway along, or forget the punchline? After that happened a couple of times, did you stop trying to tell jokes? That may be a good idea, or you may be deleting a potentially valuable tool from your communication repertoire.

Here are some suggestions for using stories and other support material well:

* Consider if the material will help make a point, or if it's just used to amuse. Either is OK for the right situation. Know your strengths; relating a personal experience or a recent news item may be better for you than an item from the Internet.

* Assess whether the audience will understand or appreciate the comment. Many speakers have found that a joke that is hilarious in Chicago is a flop in Milan.

* For oral delivery, practice the story so you can tell it smoothly and with the right effects. For an important business event, you may want to test the material with an astute reviewer.

* With the real audience, speak it "trippingly from the tongue," with good projection, clarity, pacing, and drama.

* Gauge the response. Did you get the desired reaction? (If they didn't laugh, no, don't tell it again.) If it didn't work so well, determine why not and do better the next time.

 201

Will the Spirits Come When You Need Them?

GLENDOWER I can call spirits from the vasty deep.

HOTSPUR Why so can I, or so can any man:
But will they come when you do call for them?

Henry IV, Part 1. 3, 1

In the passage above, Hotspur came up with what's called a gotcha. He called Glendower on his lofty claim, which he clearly couldn't back up.

Is your support for your position credible? Are your facts tainted? Are you blowing smoke? Have your quotations been adjusted to fit your purpose? (OK, guilty as charged. Maybe one or two of the Bard's quotes herein have been slightly tuned to make my points.)

The devil can cite Scripture for his purpose.

Antonio, *The Merchant of Venice*. 1, 3

Many people regularly cite chapter and verse from the Bible to support their position. Slave owners before the Civil War found ample justification for the righteousness of their cause in the Bible; in fact, ministers pointed out why it was the sensible way of living. Surprise—the abolitionists used the same source in their arguments to end slavery.

"You might be interested to know that the Scriptures are on our side on this," said President Reagan, defending his arms buildup program.

Are You Relying on Sound Argument or Just Sound?

> Your reasons at dinner have been sharp and sententious,
>   pleasant without scurrility, witty without affectation,
>   audacious without impudency, learned without
>   opinion, and strange without heresy.
>
> Nathaniel, *Love's Labour's Lost.* 5, 1

We're in an era where reasoned debate of issues is often omitted. Listen to many talk radio shows, and you'll find that the hosts are most affable if they find the caller's position much like their own. But watch the tenor change when someone with a different point of view calls in. Frequently the host, with the power of the program and the squelch button, interrupts the discourse of the caller, often with a raised voice and an incredulous manner. Fortunately, a few programs that value clear thinking and reasoned discourse still exist; PBS's *Talk of the Nation* noon radio program is a good example.

> Seal up the mouth of outrage for awhile,
> Till we can clear these ambiguities.
>
> Prince, *Romeo and Juliet.* 5, 3

In many daytime talk shows the key to high ratings is to have people cross the line of civilized standards of discussion and wallop the other party (and sometimes the host, such as when Geraldo Rivera ended up with a broken nose). Even what might be expected to be a higher level of discourse (e.g., among journalists or well-informed partisans) often ends up as a contest of who can shout the loudest, rather than an opportunity for each party to make his or her case. This approach is not especially new, as evidenced by this pair of astute observers:

* Cicero: "When you have no basis for an argument, abuse the plaintiff."

* Jonathan Swift, in *Gulliver's Travels*, discussing lawyers: "In pleading, they studiously avoid entering into the merits of the case; but are loud, violent and tedious in dwelling upon all circumstances which are not to the purpose."

Does the Audience Share Your Great Wit?

> A jest's prosperity lies in the ear
> Of him that hears it, never in the tongue
> Of him that makes it.
>
> Rosaline, *Love's Labour's Lost*. 5, 2

Humor can be a powerful communication device. What about ethnic humor? Dirty jokes? Sexist cartoons? *Playboy* centerfold visual aids? Most of these were standard fare in meetings a few decades back, but are guaranteed trouble today. Be careful that your so-called wit doesn't backfire.

The list of casualties is long of people who used examples they thought were funny or thought-provoking but which the audience found offensive. The wise communicator learns to review material from multiple perspectives, tests it with others, and applies the old dictum "If in doubt, leave it out." Here are a few public figures whose choice of examples got them into trouble:

* Jerry Falwell's pointing to a suspicious character on PBS's *Teletubbies* as part of a gay agenda

* Clarence Thomas's "harmless" office repartee with Anita Hill

* Tom Leech's use of a cartoon, cleverly making a point about right and left brain differences, from *Playboy* magazine

Take-Away Ideas

* Stories and other methods can draw on the audience's senses for powerful effect.

* Apply the key words "for example" to add support to your messages.

* Use material carefully so it doesn't backfire.

Part V

❧

The Medium Supports the Message

Hamlet, Prince of Denmark. 5, 1

Visual aids play a key role in business communication, allowing added dimensions via props, models, displays, and real objects. Then comes the setting, the setup, and the equipment. In the next two chapters we examine how you can add to your communication effectiveness by wise use of the medium.

Chapter 17

❧ 🕮 ❧

Alas, Poor Yorick:
Apply Visual Aids Well

To see sad sights moves more than hear them told.

The Rape of Lucrece. 1324

You can readily interweave with your information a variety of visual aids: chalkboard sketches, architectural drawings, color slides, multi-image projections, video, and more. Additional dimensions are achievable with props, models, displays, and real objects. How to use these well is the topic of this chapter.

A Picture's Worth a Thousand Words, Sometimes

Dost thou love pictures? We will fetch thee straight
Adonis painted by a running brook.

Servant, The Taming of the Shrew. Induction, 2

When used well—a definite caveat—visuals can add significantly to the success of communication for many purposes: presentations, training, new employee orientations, new product introductions, and so on.

❧ 209 ❧

In the fast-food era the use of visuals in general society continues to rise. Advertisers, packagers, newspapers, and annual reports are now big on pictures. *USA Today* achieved quick success in large part because of its extensive use of color pictures, graphs, and visual displays. The comics pages are among the most widely read sections of the paper, at least at my breakfast table.

Some visuals that have grabbed audiences and helped them understand quickly:

* To an employee suggestion committee notorious for applying the "Not Invented Here" policy to new ideas, an engineer opened his presentation with a cartoon showing a medieval general engaged in battle against a force of archers that refuse to talk to a peddler hawking . . . a Gatling gun. Picture that.

* In a seminar, a financial advisor displayed a graph that showed the retirement income levels and numbers of people in each category. A large segment was below the poverty line. We listened after that.

* Immediately following the successful attack by the United Nations forces in the 1991 Iraqi war, General Norman Schwarzkopf used a series of poster boards in his explanation of strategy, actions, and outcomes. The briefing was well-received and the video widely played.

* While not common on the campaign trail, a candidate can apply business communication methods to the campaign, as well as charts and pointers, which Ross Perot did in his run for the presidency. Some pundits credited this strategy for winning over voters.

The caveat is that simply inserting visuals into your program doesn't guarantee improved communication. With all the visuals used in today's business world, it's good to keep a pair of binoculars on hand to read the on-screen material and a machete to cut through all the information. I've been in meetings where audience members forced to endure bad slides prayed for the projector bulb to blow.

Many people tuned in to watch the 1999 Clinton impeachment hearings. Both sides used posters to display their various documents. With typically 50 lines per chart, most were impossible to read even with close-up video cameras, let alone from across the hearing room.

> Let me know the point.
>
> Claudio, *Measure for Measure.* 3, 1

To create visuals that enhance rather than impede communication, apply these basic keys:

* Make them easily readable—that is, by the audience—with adequate type sizes and color choices (both common sources of intense aggravation among viewers).

* Focus key information by omitting nonuseful clutter.

* Apply visual power by using illustrations or relationship layouts as opposed to constant bullet charts (such as this list).

* Make sure every chart clearly supports a basic point.

* Proof all charts to catch errors before the audience does.

* Bounce your visuals off colleagues or objective coaches to see if you're on the right track.

* Test them with the actual audiovisual gear and room setup.

Stir Them with Motion

Things in motion sooner catch the eye
Than what stirs not.

Ulysses, *Troilus and Cressida*. 3, 3

Communicators have a wide range of visual-aid options. Video and film are widely used for instruction, presentations, problem analysis, sales demos, and conferences. Computer graphics software and hardware can provide the same capabilities. The dynamic nature of these media can provide more realism, heighten interest compared with static visuals, and show objects in motion or change.

The value of motion was shown with the city of San Diego's winning of the 1996 Republican Convention. Some members of the selection committee had reservations about the size and sightlines of the facility. The marketing team developed a computer virtual simulation to display planned setup, seating, and viewing angles; this was noted as key to alleviating concerns and winning the convention.

With technology continually evolving, computer graphics options are readily available to add motion and other effects to communication vehicles. It's also tempting to get carried away with all the possible special effects. My advice: Be judicious in your use of computer effects, they can backfire when, instead of enhancing communication, they become distracting and perceived as gimmicky. Know your audience and environment to keep from making costly mistakes.

Hard to Beat a Good Skull, or Other Prop

Alas, poor Yorick. I knew him, Horatio, a fellow of
infinite jest, of most excellent fancy.

Hamlet, *Hamlet*. 5, 1

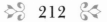

Audiences have looked forward to seeing Hamlet stroke poor Yorick's skull on the stage for centuries. Staples of safety lectures, training programs, and sales presentations are demos, role plays, simulations, and props. To get some ideas, watch those master practitioners of props and gadgetry, the hucksters at any county fair. Or tune into one of magician David Copperfield's TV specials and watch, carefully, his use of props: lions, real airplanes, the Great Wall of China. This takes a larger budget than you're likely to have.

Nutritionist Candy Cumming uses props extensively in her speaking and educational programs to dramatize her message. She mashes a loaf of white bread to reinforce the idea of low food value, displays a three-dimensional food stick showing the food values of prime rib (a lot of fat) versus chicken (less fat and more protein), and tosses confetti over food types to compare nutritional values (handfuls over fresh fruits and veggies; a few specks over fast food). These make her points stand out far stronger than just talking about them or showing pictures or graphs, plus people recall the props (and the messages) years later.

In the political realm, a key gimmick for Jesse Ventura's upset victory in the 1999 Minnesota governor's race, playing on his occupation of pro wrestler and underdog, was his foot-high action doll fighting the special interests, which capitalized on one of his campaign themes.

One of the beauties of props is that they may be readily available and cost little. "Seven-year-old Juan House of Southcrest made some San Diego City Council members squirm yesterday. His friends showed members of the Council's Natural Resources Committee gallon-sized plastic bags filled with hundreds of cigarette butts that had been dug out of the sand in tot lots at four city playgrounds." Juan told of how smaller kids play with the butts and even eat them. This persuasive band convinced the committee to unanimously vote for the drafting of an ordinance to ban smoking in or near tot lots.

The beauty of this sinful dame
Made many princes thither frame
To seek her as a bedfellow,
In marriage-pleasures playfellow:
Which to prevent he made a law,
To keep her still and men in awe,
That whoso asked her for his wife,
Hid riddle told not, lost his life:
So for her many a wight [suitor] did die,
As yon grim looks do testify.

Gower, Pericles. 1, Chorus

If one skull is good, why not a whole display case of them? What "yon grim looks" refers to are heads of suitors who failed the riddle test. I would have thought the display provided a strong signal that this maiden was not one to approach without careful consideration, and yet they kept coming forward. Was she that good, or was it the challenge as represented by those props?

While on a camping vacation in British Columbia, I saw a memorable presentation as part of the evening campfire program. The ranger kept the group involved by bringing in a variety of props as he explained how glaciers are formed and make their way across the landscape. His props were all made from low-cost, readily available materials; with diligent preparation, everything worked as intended. We listened, enjoyed, learned, and remembered (even a year later); the props, plus a high-energy delivery, were key.

Add Another Element: Hands-on Experience

He [Orlando] sent me thither, stranger as I am,
To tell you his story, that you might excuse

His broken promise, and to give you this napkin,
Dyed in his blood.
(*Rosalind swoons*)

Oliver, As You Like It. 4, 3

Oliver has brought in another of the Bard's staples: the bloody cloth. This hands-on gimmick from—trust me—a comedy has a powerful effect. It adds another dimension to sensory experience by expanding from hear-and-see to active participation and experiential learning— the old kick-the-tires syndrome. Hands-on products or activities often affect audiences far more than static visuals. At trade shows the most sure-fire attraction is the popcorn machine, whose scents lure attendees from the far corners of the auditorium (at least it works with me).

Or, with the rest, where is your darling Rutland?
Look, York: I stained this napkin with the blood
That valiant Clifford, with his rapier's point,
Made issue from the bosom of the boy;
And if thine eyes can water for his death,
I give thee this to dry thy cheeks withal.

Queen Margaret, Henry VI, Part 3. 1, 4

Some managers in Japan apparently saw value in this sort of experiential activity for motivating subordinates, as noted in a report about a departed young executive. What contributed to his suicide, and to those of many other young hard-driving or driven professionals, at a young age? "It may have been the abusive bosses who forced him and other junior employees to drink beer from the shoes of senior managers."

(*Enter the King with a supplication, and the Queen with
Suffolk's head . . .*)

> Oft have I heard that grief softens the mind,
> And makes it fearful and degenerate.
> Think therefore on revenge and cease to weep.
> But who can cease to weep and look on this?
> Here may his head lie on my throbbing breast:
> But where's the body that I should embrace?

> Queen Margaret, *King Henry VI, Part 2.* 4, 4

Here we have one more skull, but this one becomes a moving prop, in more ways than one. The Duke of Suffolk, a notorious high-level conniver, was caught at his game and banished from England. He was captured by pirates, who naturally chopped off his head. They gave the parts (body and head, separated) to a prisoner and set him free. Being a considerate chap, he delivered the parts to the Queen. As she had been having a long-term illicit romance with the Duke, she becomes heavily distraught, to the point of carrying his head around for a while (though she did yearn for the rest of him). Wouldn't that scene have made an impact on anyone who passed her in the hall?

> Kind souls, what weep you when you but behold
> Our Caesar's vesture wounded? Look you here,
> Here is himself, marr'd, as you see, with traitors.

> Mark Antony, *Julius Caesar.* 3, 2

If a skull is good, why not a whole body, especially one with a few slices in it? Remember the movie *Weekend at Bernie's?* Bernie was a complete body, who, though recently departed, kept appearing at inopportune moments.

So, when planning your props, be creative. Use your head; explore the whole body of available options.

Don't Gild the Lily

To gild refined gold, to paint the lily,
To throw a perfume on the violet,
To smooth the ice, or add another hue
Unto the rainbow, or with taper-light
To seek the beauteous eye of heaven to garnish,
Is wasteful and ridiculous excess.

Salisbury, King John. 4, 2

Visual aids and effects can be helpful in communication, but can backfire if overdone. Are there any computer graphics practitioners in your work environment? Probably plenty, as computer-based presentations are staples in conference rooms all over the world. These tools have greatly increased productivity in preparing and displaying material.

Actually, Moses seemed to do OK with a couple of stone tablets and someone's powerful marker. For college lectures, it was the chalkboards (and occasionally the flying eraser). For meetings, it was flip charts, viewgraphs, and color slides. They all did the job, but getting high quality was tedious and took experts. Today anybody with access to a computer is a graphics developer.

More matter, with less art.

Queen, Hamlet. 2, 2

However, having better technology and using that technology wisely do not automatically go hand in hand. Having a good tool doesn't ensure a good product. I can buy the same tools as a plumber and still botch the job (in fact, I have). Graphics can still be unreadable, unfathomable, and distracting.

According to an article in *The Wall Street Journal*, the Pentagon's top brass declared, "Enough of the bells and whistles . . . the Venetian-blind effects. . . . All we need is the information." (This is the same lament as the Queen's, referring to the excess of "art" at the expense of "matter.") The ones with the information are over-doing the options available with computers, and turning out material that is interfering with understanding. Here the old Marshall Mc-Luhan adage transforms to "The medium becomes (or overwhelms) the message." Use the technology to your advantage and to the meeting's benefit, but resist the urge to get too gimmicky, as it may be a waste of your valuable time and hurt your cause.

For a major presentation, the graphics staff had designed a whole raft of special effects to accompany the computerized visuals. When the speakers started practicing with these, it was clear that the effects were interfering with their timing and ability to focus the messages. So, at a critical rehearsal point, all progress stopped while the graphics people spent hours removing most of the effects they thought would add to the overall value.

Are Your Props Warped?

Thy best props are warped.

Daughter, *The Two Noble Kinsmen*. 3, 2

Courtroom attorneys, both the TV and real kind, are fond of using demos and props to sway juries. Remember the O. J. Simpson trial, which riveted much of the nation for weeks? Remember the glove demo, which backfired on the prosecution when the glove wouldn't fit the hand of Mr. Simpson? Remember the theme hammered home by the defense: "If it doesn't fit, you must acquit"? That one demo settled the trial.

Here's one more communicator whose use of props backfired at a huge cost.

> AMBASSADOR   He [the Dauphin] therefore sends you,
>   meeter for your spirit, This tun of treasure . . .
>
> KING   What treasures, uncle?
>
> EXETER   Tennis-balls, my liege.
>
> KING   . . . Tell the pleasant Prince this mock of his
> Hath turn'd his balls to gun-stones, and his soul
> Shall stand sore charged for the wasteful vengeance
> That shall fly with them; for many a thousand widows
> Shall this his mock mock out of their dear husbands.
>
> *Henry V.* 1, 2

This prop went awry, as the Dauphin's gift, the tennis balls, infuriated the King. The war, which might have been averted with a more respectful communiqué, was on. France lost. Bad move, Dauphin.

When planning props, demos, and hands-on exercises, make sure you've planned carefully. Test them to verify that they will work as intended. Get there well ahead of the audience so you can place the props for easy use. In general, keep the prop out of sight until you want to use it; a prop in clear view can be a big distraction. Do not pass your props around the audience, which is a bigger distraction.

Take-Away Ideas

* Visual aids add dimension and power to communication.
* Use visual support wisely.

* For extra punch, incorporate a skull, body, or other hands-on gadget.

* Make sure these props work.

For true Shakespeare fans, here's more about his wide use of the skull as prop.

> (Reenter one with the heads [*of two lords upon two poles*]
> But is not this braver? Let them kiss one another, for they loved well when they were alive. [*The heads are made to touch one another*]. Now part them again, lest they consult about the giving up of some more towns in France. Soldiers, defer the spoil of the city until night, for with these borne before us, instead of maces, will we ride through the streets; and at every corner have them kiss. Away!
>
> Jack Cade, *Henry VI, Part 2*. 4, 7

Having seen the dramatic power of one skull, Shakespeare here went for two—moving at that—with Cade's own soon to meet the slicer. Let's keep these props coming, with a phrase you've all heard.

> Off with his head, and set it on York gates;
> So York may overlook the town of York.
>
> Queen Margaret, *Henry VI, Part 3*. 1, 4

So York's head, delivered by Clifford, is the prop on display. Stay tuned.

Off with the traitor's head,
　　And rear it in the place your father's stands.

Warwick, *Henry VI, Part 3*. 2, 6

The tide has turned; now it's Clifford's head that goes up and York's that comes down. Isn't this exciting? Nothing like changing props, though you need a scorecard to keep track of who's coming up to the post next.

Chapter 18

Silence That Dreadful Bell!
Use the Medium Wisely

> This castle hath a pleasant seat: the air
> Nimbly and sweetly recommends itself
> Unto our gentle senses.
>
> Duncan (King of Scotland), *Macbeth*. 1, 6

In this chapter we'll examine not the content of our communications but the medium through which they are conducted. We'll start with the setting for communication—the facility—and the arrangements. We'll explore the world of communications technology and how you can better apply hardware and software methodologies to enhance the effectiveness of your communication. We'll also point out some of the problems of technology that impede communication.

In the old days communication was done by voice, ear, eye, and sometimes club. Then along came drums, smoke signals, and the telephone. Today communication is often done via e-mail, computer graphics, and videoconferencing (along with voice, ear, eye, and sometimes club).

Is Your Castle Pleasant?

> And here's a marvelous convenient place for our
> rehearsal.
>
> Quince, *Midsummer Night's Dream.* 3, 1

What sort of facilities do you work in? Do your offices, cubicles, or conference rooms have pleasant seats and sweet air? And does that have anything to do with getting the job done? Do your facilities facilitate or impede?

The conference room is the usual facility for many types of communication: team meetings, classes, program reviews, presentations, negotiations. If the room is well laid out and outfitted, that alone can expedite communication. (Or a knife in the ribs, which is what happened to Duncan in Macbeth's castle.)

> I think this be the most villainous house in all London
> road for fleas.
>
> Second carrier, *Henry IV, Part 1.* 2, 1

What has your experience been with less-than-helpful meeting facilities? Ever attend any events and wish someone had been a bit more careful setting up the room, or even deciding whether to use it at all? Take a look at the conference rooms where you work. Do they expedite or interfere with success? Besides fleas, the list of common gripes is long: too hot (or too cold), poor lighting, bad chairs, outside distractions, inadequate power outlets, cold coffee (and no decaf or latte) to name a few.

> It strikes a man more dead than a great reckoning in a
> little room.
>
> Touchstone, *As You Like It.* 3, 3

Facilities can be a key consideration in high-level meetings, involving such factors as location, room layout, attendees, and refreshments.

In 1969, shortly after President Nixon's inauguration, his administration initiated the Vietnam peace talks. "A dispute over the size and shape of the table to be used during the proceedings further held up the expanded talks for ten weeks."

Move forward to the 2000 presidential campaign, where a major debate issue was the setup, with Al Gore wanting the debaters to stand on the podium and George W. Bush pushing for sitting at a table. The resolution? Debate 1 had both standing, and debate 2 had both sitting behind a table.

I was coaching for a major presentation to an admiral and staff. When I visited the room, it was obvious to me that the chairs were uncomfortable and of mediocre quality. I pointed this out to the team leader, who immediately concurred and replaced them with "admiral-level chairs." Then I checked the overhead projector (this was back in the stone age, folks) and noted it had several scratches. Once again, they immediately agreed and replaced the projector. Because they had been using the facilities regularly, they had missed these deficiencies, which were obvious to an outside observer. (See the kind of astute advice a high-priced consultant can impart?)

Consider the Meeting Environment

And, if we meet, we shall not 'scape a brawl;
For now these hot days is the mad blood stirring.

Benvolio, *Romeo and Juliet*. 3, 1

The importance of meeting room temperature and environment was clearly illustrated in a job I once had in Ohio . . . in July. The department had a weekly series of educational programs, with truly good speakers coming to us via training films. The meetings were at 3 P.M., the room was not air-conditioned, and slides were shown, so the room was dark. With most of us taking a weekly afternoon siesta, how useful was the program?

> This house is but a butchery;
> Abhor it, fear it, do not enter it!
>
> Adam, *As You Like It.* 2, 3

Later, as a corporate ombudsman, I heard daily from employees about problems they wanted solved, and that their own management had done little about. Probably the major category of lament was "It's too hot in our area" or "We're freezing over here." Another, related category pertained to air quality—no circulation, or the BO of the person in the next cubicle (which the boss would do nothing about because it was such a personal, sensitive issue). As many requests surfaced to limit smoking in the workplace, I was given the task of developing a policy—partly because of my role, but also because no one else wanted to touch it. Few organizations had any smoking policies at that time. With much awareness of the issue's sensitivity, we came out with a policy whose most-welcomed provision limited smoking in meetings. Now, a couple of decades later, entire buildings are off limits to smoking.

Cover the "Toil and Trouble"

WITCHES Double, double toil and trouble;
Fire burn and cauldron bubble.

SECOND WITCH Fillet of a fenny snake,
In the caldron boil and bake;

Eye of newt and toe of frog,
Wool of bat and tongue of dog,
Adder's fork and blind-worm's sting,
Lizard's leg and howlet's wing,
For a charm of powerful trouble,
Like a hell-broth boil and bubble.

Macbeth. 4, 1

For many communication forms, a variety of details need to be addressed to ensure a smooth, trouble-free engagement. For a group meeting, if you're the person in charge of the details, you may delegate this—do this cautiously—but if something goes wrong, you deserve the blame (if it goes right, no one notices). You can imagine what those famous witches had to do in advance to make sure the meeting would succeed: you can't just get eye of newt from the office supply cabinet.

It is Othello's pleasure, our noble and valiant general,
that upon certain tidings now arrived, . . . every man
put himself into triumph; some to dance, some to
make bonfires, each man to what sport and revels his
addition leads him. . . . All offices are open, and
there is full liberty of feasting.

Herald, *Othello.* 2, 2

Easy for him to say. What about the details to make sure all this revelry would actually happen? Do we need a band? Where's the wood for the bonfires? If it's your meeting, I strongly suggest preparing a detailed checklist of everything that will be required; then keep checking it to make sure all is ready. One more thing: Remember the power of Murphy's Law, which has the uncanny ability to become operable in business meetings. It's funny, maybe, when someone else messes up; it's painful and often costly when you do.

Think carefully about the facility and setting, such as table arrangement, seating comfort, temperature control, lighting, and audiovisual needs.

Not paying attention to details can show up in strange places. During the 2000 Summer Olympics in Sydney, Australia, one of the big embarrassments occurred during the gymnastics competition. Halfway through the women's all around program, someone finally realized the vaulting horse had not been set to the proper height, throwing off several of the world's top gymnasts.

The FBI charged four men with a scheme to fraudulently obtain $1.6 million in gold from a metal products manufacturer, Stern-Leach Company. The company smelled a rat when it was contacted by one of the four, who identified himself as "Sargent Michael Jeffries" of the U.S. Department of Defense. Maybe he should have spelled "sergeant" correctly. Could Woody Allen have written a better script? (I refer you back to Chapter 1.)

Media Options Are Changing Fast

> Call you this gamut? tut, I like it not;
> Old fashions please me best; I am not so nice
> To change true rules for odd inventions.
>
> Bianca, *The Taming of the Shrew.* 3, 1

In setting the medium of communication you have a wide range of options, from basic to intricate. Much communication is done by two people discussing a topic; throw in a telephone and you're using an added medium. With that you have the advantage of being able to communicate while separated along with the disadvantages of losing facial expressions, possible static on the line, and hitting a telephone pole when using your cell phone while driving.

For many formal communications, such as speeches, the primary medium is the voice. Mark Antony did fine with that medium, as did Jesus on the Mount and Abe Lincoln with his Gettysburg Address. Today any audience over about 25 requires a public address system, plus, for distance communication, radio, video, Internet, and whatever's next. Since television and satellites came onto the scene, events have been experienced live, worldwide, and from the moon. Recall that live "giant step for mankind."

New media for workplace communication are being adopted at a hectic pace: yesterday the mail carrier, today cell phones, pagers, Palm Pilots, and e-mail. Your conferences may use multiscreen computer-based graphics, online multisite interactions, simultaneous translations, and even instantaneous audience response systems replacing the thumbs-up/thumbs-down voting system. You also have a wide range of visual media at your disposal, from flip charts, posters, and overhead projectors to higher-tech computer-based projection systems and videoconferences.

Stay Current or Fade Fast

> Why is my verse so barren of new pride,
> So far from variation or quick change?
> Why with the time do I not glance aside
> To new-found methods and to compounds strange?
>
> *Sonnet 76*

What communication technologies are you using on a regular basis? As a new advance arrives, do you embrace it or resist it?

Maybe you recall when telephone prefixes were letters or words, such as "Pennsylvania 6-5000," a Glenn Miller hit back in the telephone stone age. When the shift to numbered prefixes arrived, many people fought it vigorously, mounting outraged calls to the phone companies, letter campaigns to the Federal Communications Commission, and probably lawsuits.

With the arrival of each new technology, some grasp it eagerly while others resist and belittle it. Some years back I attended a computer show and saw the then new Apple Macintosh computer. I dismissed it quickly as a cute machine that would perhaps be good for games. A few million sales later, I guess it does have a place. Sometimes I'm a slow learner; I had the same reaction when I saw my first Palm Pilot. Cute, but who needs it?

> O Chief! The day is lost, all is lost!
> (O Seigneur! Le jour est perdu, tout est perdu!)
>
> Duke of Orleans, *Henry V.* 4, 5

Why was the day lost? Because the French duke's team, with five times the forces, had just been mopped up by Henry's English team. This occurred because the English, knowing the terrain was wet and boggy, were smarter in their choice of methodology, relying on easily mobile archers with longbows to wipe out the heavily armored, mounted French knights who could barely move. (For a complete analysis, read *Asimov's Guide to Shakespeare,* Wing Books, 1970).

A few centuries later the British would have serious problems of their own against lesser-equipped forces—recall those highly visible Redcoats marching together across the meadows while the scruffy-uniformed American revolutionaries fired away from the woods.

So are you using the best technology for your communication requirements? Today's businesspeople use daily a wide range of communication systems that have added hugely to their capability. One of my first jobs out of high school was as an airline reservations agent. All day long I took phone calls from customers and advised them about flight routes and availabilities. This was all precomputer, so our primary communication technology was color-coded, wall-mounted flight numbers. Actually, we were extremely efficient, with eye, brain, and mouth nearly instantaneously assessing and conveying information. However, for reservations a week away, involving connecting flights and special fares, the process slowed w-a-a-y down.

Today all that is done with the help of a computer, and many people go online and cut out the agents entirely. Wonderful capability. On the other hand (with technology always comes a caveat), have you tried to get a reservation or trip information when those dreaded words come out "The computer is down"?

With the wonders of the Internet, I can review electronic presentations sent to me from across the continent via e-mail, and get comments back almost as fast as if I were present in the conference room where these are being honed (and perhaps more efficiently, without the hubbub of a group meeting in process). With electronic conferencing, we're all communicating together from a half-dozen locations.

Adapting to new communication techniques typically requires some start-up outlays and a few trials before efficient operation and the resultant benefits are achieved. Is it worth the trouble? If the current methods work fine, perhaps not. A lot of excellent communication is being done with the lowly overhead projector. However, in a competitive environment, trying to win over management or customers may dictate using more current technologies. Applying Marshall McLuhan's "the medium is the message" means that audiences may perceive yours is a stodgy outfit on the basis of your failure to use computer-based systems.

Technology Can Backfire

Silence that dreadful bell: it frights the isle
From her propriety.

Othello, *Othello* 2, 3

 231

With technology sometimes comes abuse of the gadgetry. Automated phone systems are one of the worst culprits. In the old days when you called a company, you got to talk to a real live person. Have you called your bank lately, the doctor's office, Company ABC, or, horrors, the complaint department? It's not unusual to spend five minutes on the phone just working your way through the options, or to be put on hold for twenty minutes listening to rap radio before getting kicked off the system, followed by your screaming "*&%$##$^**&^%.!!!"

Cell phones have become a staple of communication at the office and on the road. Have you perchance seen one or two articles about the abuse of cell phones? Have you seen the *Car Talk* guys' bumper stickers saying "Drive Now, Talk Later"? Have you ever been irritated while dining in a fine restaurant and having to listen to the chap in the next booth loudly carrying on a detailed conversation?

While cell phones have become a valuable communication device, they've also become a major irritant at meetings, presentations, and even theater productions. I was enjoying a comedy troupe at a small theater when a loud "beep . . . beep" went off, disrupting the routine on stage. The actor stopped the scene, and everyone looked for the culprit, who was the fellow sitting next to me, up in the cheap seats. One wonders what the Bard would have done about the cell phone problem—maybe "Silence that dreadful bell, thou gross watery pumpion!" (For help in selecting insults, see Chapter 21.)

Many events now open with a stern request to shut off the cell phones. In my hometown the mayor was holding a press conference to announce a new policy requiring the shutting off of these disturbing gadgets, when—take a guess—her cell phone went off. This had three immediate effects: It was a big embarrassment, it vividly showed the pervasiveness of the problem, and it got more press than a trouble-free conference could have gotten.

Here's a word to the wise. If you're going to be over in Saudi Arabia on a business trip, be *very* careful about where you use that cell phone.

A Saudi army captain found out the hard way that when the flight crew on a plane about to take off says to not use the cell phone, they really, really mean it. He ignored the order, whereupon he was pulled off the plane and hauled before a judge. The sentence: 70 lashes.

Remember You're in Murphy's Realm

> O, what a scene of foolery have I seen,
> Of sighs, of groans, of sorrow, and of teen
> [aggravation]!
>
> Biron, *Love's Labour's Lost*. 4, 3

At the annual shareholders meeting of Lockheed Corporation, a high-tech company, the chairman was in the middle of the all-important slide presentation when—tada!—the projector went ka-flooie. As he started to add some levity, the public address system quit. One of those days, I guess.

How often have you experienced such breakdowns in your business communications? When it happens to someone else, it can be amusing; if it happens to you, it is embarrassing and, as in this case, costly. The program stops, adjustments have to be made, and productivity grinds to a halt. While acts of nature sometimes are truly the cause of the problem, far, far more often Murphy's Law problems can be prevented by application of another old saw: the Devil is in the details.

Perhaps you've read about the well-publicized visits by Murphy during important events involving Bill Gates, Bill Clinton, presidents Ford and Carter together . . . it's a long list.

> And oftentimes excusing of a fault
> Doth make the fault the worse by the excuse.
>
> Pembroke, *King John*. 4, 2

Have you ever goofed in the middle of an important presentation, meeting, or dialogue? Brain quit, forgot the punchline, was obviously poorly prepared, had the bulb burn out? When something does go wrong, a common mistake is to get flustered, apologize (for your incompetence?), blame the fates (or a subordinate), and get thrown off course. What this usually does is call attention to the problem, which others may not even be aware of (though it is hard not to notice when the bulb burns out). Better to accept what happened, make a quick decision about what to do next, and get it done.

Have you backed up that file lately?

Let's Further Think—of Backups

> Let's further think of this;
> Weigh what convenience both of time and means
> May fit us to our shape: if this should fail,
> And that our drift look through our bad performance,
> 'Twere better not assay'd: therefore this project
> Should have a back or second.
>
> King Claudius, *Hamlet*. 4, 7

A team had prepared thoroughly for a key high-tech presentation to a contract review board. On the final preparation day they made several trials, with the laptop computer/projector system working smoothly. The next day they walked into the conference room, turned on the gear, and nothing worked. The clock was ticking, so after a quick assessment they shifted to their backup—old-fashioned paper copy—thus saving a critical meeting.

In planning for your engagement, such as a meeting you are chairing, where any equipment will be involved, consider where having a backup would be good insurance. Review the setup and identify any potential failures that would severely impact meeting productivity and success. Some candidates:

* *Projectors*. If the bulb fails, where is the spare? Can you get it immediately, and do you know how to replace the old one? I've seen meetings come to a standstill while several people race from office to office looking for a bulb, which, once found, wouldn't work. Huge embarrassment.

* *Computers*. For significant meetings, it's a comfortable feeling to know you're prepared in case computer 1 goes down. Try out the switching process in advance. What's your option when the remote doesn't work?

* *Laser pointers*. Spare batteries are always a good idea.

* *Travel itinerary or method*. How are you getting across town? What if that flight is canceled? What's plan B?

Adolf Hitler knew the importance of having a backup. According to Sergei Mironenko, Director of Russia's State Archives, at Hitler's final moment in that Berlin bunker, he used two suicide methods simultaneously. Method A was a cyanide capsule; method B was a bullet in the mouth. The autopsy showed method A did the job, but just in case . . .

For the Shakespeare fans, here's the rest of the Hamlet story. Did Claudius's team settle for just the one backup? No. Was Claudius's backup plan called into play? Yes. Did it work as intended? Read on.

Laertes is to have a friendly fencing match with Hamlet, with both using dull blades. However, Laertes will actually use a sharp blade. The backup is poison on the tip, so just a nick will finish him off. But his co-conspirator, Claudius, wants more insurance.

> I'll have prepared him
> A chalice for the nonce, whereon but sipping,

If he by chance escape your venom'd stuck,
Our purpose may hold there.

King Claudius, *Hamlet*. 4, 7

Another backup! Does the melancholy Dane have a chance against two such scoundrels? Here's the thirty-second summary. Laertes' first plan runs into trouble because he fails to nip Hamlet. During a break he launches a sneak attack and does give him the fatal nick. Hamlet now realizes Laertes' blade is sharp, not dull, so he does a fast blade swap and sticks it to Laertes. What about the other backup, the poisoned drink? Another snafu, as Hamlet's dear old mum downs that, unaware it's poisoned. With Laertes' dying words, he blows the whistle on the mastermind of this whole plot, Claudius. So Hamlet forces Claudius also to sip the poisoned drink. (Was Mel Brooks wrong when he said, "It's good to be the king"?) All die.

Still, remember, it's good to have backups.

Don't Let the Medium Become the Message

The evil men do lives after them;
The good is oft interred with their bones.

Mark Antony, *Julius Caesar*. 3, 2

I often ask seminar participants to recall some Murphy's Law problem that happened to someone else—the squealing mic, upside-down slide, collapsed posterboard. They readily can recall with amusement the details of something that happened perhaps two decades before. What about the content or results of the meeting or presentation? No memory at all. We can vividly recall the screw-up—the evil—but can't recall anything about the content—the good.

We have kiss'd away
Kingdoms and provinces.

Scarus, *Antony and Cleopatra.* 3, 10

Don't let your objective be lost because of failure to attend the little things.

Take-Away Ideas

* The medium plays a large part in communication success.

* Pay attention to facilities and environment.

* Used well technology can add to productivity and results; used badly it can backfire.

* Anticipate potential problems and be ready with backups.

Part VI

—❧—

Competitive Communication

Coriolanus. 5, 3

In this segment we look at the competitive aspects of communication. There are many situations in which you go after something tangible: a contract, the go-ahead for a pet research project, infusion of capital, promotion, an extra month of vacation . . .

We'll offer ways to form up your own team and head off the competing Brand X bunch, and we'll suggest how to handle success or setback. Advance clue: Don't take parts of this too seriously.

Chapter 19

Gather Your Team: Once More
unto the Breach!

We few, we happy few, we band of brothers;
For he today that sheds his blood with me
Shall be my brother.

King Henry, *Henry V.* 4, 3

Communicating in business today is done as often by teams as by one person. Tiger teams, task forces, and IPTs (integrated project teams) have become standard fare for major programs. These are made up of people from various departments, specialties, and levels. They may involve people from several companies as well as the customers.

Road shows, annual conferences, political campaigns, even forays into battle almost always require teams. Beside the principal party or primary experts for specific areas, the team may include other people contributing to the task, such as content support, graphics specialists, cost analysts, reviewers, and even consultants (above all, don't forget them).

What a Team!

You that will fight,
Follow me close; I'll bring you to't.

Antony, Antony and Cleopatra. 4, 4

Even if yours is basically a one-person operation, it's still wise to stop and reflect on what resources will be required, or might add to making the job go smoothly, before you get far along in preparation. Would delegating the preparation of required materials to a computer specialist take pressure off yourself and achieve a better product? Would it be worth a call to SCORE (Senior Corps of Retired Executives) or a local Chamber of Commerce research specialist to get some advice or information?

My train are men of choice and rarest parts,
That all particulars of duty know,
And in the most exact regard support
The worships of their name.

Lear, King Lear. 1, 4

Teams often tackle the job at hand under difficult conditions, demanding schedules, and severe pressures. During the process, when differences arise, arguments rage, and tempers flare, it's good to know you're working with a team of competent fellow professionals. I have been part of hundreds of teams over the years. And years later, a camaraderie still exists and war stories abound from those days (especially if the project was a success). Just look around many offices, where team photos, mugs, and caps are on display from projects done twenty years ago.

Or Maybe a Motley Crew

> And now my whole charge consists of ancients,
>   corporals, lieutenants, gentlemen of companies, slaves
>   as ragged as Lazarus . . . never soldiers, but discarded
>   unjust serving-men, younger sons to younger
>   brothers, revolted tapsters, and ostlers trade-fallen . . .
>   ten times more dishonourable ragged than an old-
>   faced ancient.
>
> Falstaff, *Henry IV, Part 1*. 4, 2

Then again, sometimes the team isn't so great. The process becomes unwieldy, personalities don't work out, conflicts become evident, or you can't stand the leader or team member you are obligated to work with. You question the quality, credentials, or reliability of some of your team members.

> They say there's but five upon this isle; we art three of
>   them; if th' other two be brain'd like us, the state
>   totters.
>
> Trinculo (a jester), *The Tempest*. 3, 2

Sometimes you don't have much choice. Much as you might like an organizational divorce, it's not practical. The activity and the team continue, so you make the best of it, even though you know you've been tossed in amongst a pack of losers and incompetents—yourself excepted, of course.

> I am joined with no foot land-rakers, no long-staff
>   sixpenny strikers, none of these mad mustachio
>   purple-hued maltworms; but with nobility and

> tranquility, burgomasters and great onyers, such as
> can hold in, such as will strike sooner than speak,
> and speak sooner than drink, and drink sooner than
> pray.
>
> Gadshill, *Henry IV, Part 1*. 2, 1

Is that high praise or not?

On a Winning Team, Everybody Counts

> O wonder!
> How many goodly creatures are there here!
>
> Miranda, *The Tempest*. 5, 1

Whether in sports, debate, political campaigns, rocket launches, or
business, good teamwork is essential for success. Recall the words of
another prolific quote generator, Ben Franklin, who in 1776 pulled the
disparate American Revolutionary factions together with "Gentlemen,
we must all hang together. If not, we shall assuredly hang separately."

One of the best examples illustrating the importance of the "all
for one" spirit are the eco-challenges, five- to seven-day outdoor ad-
ventures carried out under extremely arduous conditions. If one person starts slipping, the others must adapt their styles so that person
can carry on to completion. Egos, finger pointing, cliques, sloughing
off—characteristics of a team in disarray—rarely happen in this situation because (a) everyone realizes those won't get them anywhere
and (b) the roles may be reversed the next day.

> Pray heaven he be;
> For I have served him, and the man commands
> Like a full soldier.
>
> Montano, *Othello*. 2, 1

When assembling a team, choose the leader carefully. This is the person who sets the tone for the team; brings experience, knowledge, and perspective that other team members may lack; and provides direction, inspiration, and discipline to keep the team on course toward a successful conclusion. Fundamentally, the leader is a communicator.

> We cannot all be masters.
>
> Iago, Othello. 1, 1

If you are part of a team, do the best job you can at your assigned role, while also being a good team player. Keep the communication lines open with your colleagues. Whatever role you've been assigned, take the assignment seriously. But, as has been often noted, don't take yourself so seriously that it adversely affects the team. (I don't put forth Iago as one of your all-time great team players.)

Sometimes team members downplay the contributions of others lower on the organizational chart. If some members feel devalued, the team may suffer. I've found it useful to remind myself how team productivity at work would decline if each of us "big shots" had to clean our own toilets.

> O, name him not; let us not break with him,
> For he will never follow any thing
> That other men begin.
>
> Brutus, Julius Caesar. 2, 1

Every member of a team is there because he or she has a contribution to make to the team. It does the team no good if one or two individuals shine and the team, loses. Bill Russell of the Boston Celtics basketball team, which had huge success with him at center, was a prime example of a superb team contributor. His individual statistics were not overwhelming, but his combination of success in multiple categories was.

(Reenter attendant, with two murderers)

Stage directions, *Macbeth*. 3, 1

This is your team marching in for the kickoff meeting. Does this give you that comfortable warm feeling? Would you perhaps keep your eye on your wallet and laptop computer, knowing who your colleagues were? Would this activate you to sharpen that resume quickly and put in a fast call to the recruiting department of another company?

Then again, if these characters fill a key need for your team, against the opposition—Go team!

Strange Bedfellows

Alas the storm is come again! best way is to creep
under his gaberdine; there is no other shelter
hereabout: misery acquaints a man with strange
bedfellows.

Trinculo, *The Tempest*. 2, 2

Team makeup is often a compromise. Sometimes a team is staffed with people from different departments. As a team we may think we're doing perfectly fine, so why does management force these new members on us? Why do we need X, Y, or Z? Many teams are formed from several divisions of a company or from several companies. This occurs regularly in pursuing a new business opportunity, or for conferences where suppliers and users are exchanging information.

There's small choice in rotten apples.

Hortensio, Taming of the Shrew. 1, 1

It sometime occurs that your new project team, this winning combo (you hope), has been assembled from companies that have been arch-rivals on other projects—casting aspersions on one another, perhaps even suing each other. Remember the team of Richard Nixon and Nelson Rockefeller, or Jack Kennedy and LBJ?

Early in my career, my company, General Dynamics, was pursuing a huge opportunity, and our main partner was McDonnell Aircraft. Arm in arm, we would march into the conference room, a cohesive team, pals to the end, to meet with our potential customers. Meanwhile, in another conference room, our other teams—composed of our respective attorneys and supporting cast of managers, engineers, and manufacturing specialists—were suing each other for major stakes. These simultaneous engagements and affiliations prompted our corporate attorney to recall an old maxim from the legal profession: "Thou shalt not litigate by day and copulate by night"—except, of course, that's roughly, though not literally, what we were doing.

One for All, and . . .

And truly I think, if all our wits were to issue out of
one skull, they would fly east, west, north, south,
and their consent of one direct way should be at
once to all the points o' the compass.

Third citizen, Coriolanus. 2, 3

If you're the leader, keep one more role in mind: that of team builder and cheerleader. Having worked with over 200 teams during my twenty-year career as a consultant, I've seen the value a good leader can bring to a team, and I've seen how poor leaders often end up with struggling teams.

Recall Bill Murray, in the movie *Stripes*, turning a bunch of misfits into a smooth-functioning team in one of the funniest scenes in the film with a fine bit of team building.

As coach to a team pursuing a major contract, I quickly became aware that this was a group of individuals but not a team. As we went through the process of development and practice, there was little cross-support between players. I spoke with the team leader, who totally agreed, saying, "This team lacks glue. And it's time I did something about it." He had a special team meeting, with the sole topic being the necessity to pull together as a team to make a good showing. They did, the environment improved, and they won.

Another leader used a team-building technique you may want to try. The story is that New England Patriots football team coach Bill Belichick paid an offensive lineman $200 to start a fight with defender Lawyer Milloy during a practice session. A massive brawl resulted involving thirty players—offense versus defense—with a string of smaller tussles continuing through the practice. That weekend the Patriots beat the Cincinnati Bengals. Did the midweek brawl provide the emotional lift? Said one Patriot: "It was one of the best practices we've had this season. It's exactly what we needed. We played today with a lot of emotion and fire, no question." This also demonstrates the insight of Shakespeare, who, you recall, wrote, "The first thing we do, let's kill all the lawyers." (*Henry IV, Part 2*, 4, 2) (We had to get that in somewhere.)

Sometimes the leader is the obstacle. In one team, the project head was a perfectionist who was so concerned about his own role that he was spending little time with the other team members. The camaraderie was missing. I suggested they all head over to the local pub and have dinner together. A half-hour into the evening, after a beer or two, the war stories started to unfold from all parties, and it turned into a lively evening. The next morning it was a new team. We won the bid, which I doubt would have happened with the "before" team.

If a team lacks cohesiveness in meetings, reviews, presentations, or dialogues, that will be quickly picked up by decision makers. They may choose to raise this as an issue, or even worse, say nothing overtly while down-rating your team, possibly a judgment fatal to your cause.

> We ready are to try our fortunes
> To the last man.
>
> Mowbray, *Henry IV, Part 2*. 4, 2

Isn't this the sort of attitude you want your team to have as you charge that hill, tackle that tough project, or head in for the critical review? Good team building can help that happen. (On the other hand, this "last man" stuff may be an overly severe test to lay on the team.)

If It Is Broke, Fix It

> A plague upon it when thieves cannot be true to
> another!
>
> Falstaff, *Henry IV, Part 1*. 2, 2

> I do desire we be better strangers.
>
> Orlando, *As You Like It*. 3, 2

Sometimes the team just isn't working out. Partners realize their differences are too great for them to stay together. Personalities aren't meshing well. Scheduling conflicts or commitments interfere with productivity. This may be the time to change team makeup. After all . . .

Many a good hanging prevents a bad marriage.

Feste, *Twelfth Night*. 1, 5

Ready for Action: The Breech Awaits

One of the most famous scenes in Shakespeare is when Henry V urges his team of worn-out warriors onward against the French forces. This was classic team building, which led to a huge success. This is the halftime speech given by the coach when the team is behind, by the Amway team leader at the regional conference, by the keynote speaker at the national political convention. Charge!

> Once more unto the breach, dear friends, once more . . .
> But when the blast of war blows in our ears,
> Then imitate the action of the tiger;
> Stiffen the sinews, summon up the blood . . .
> Now set the teeth and stretch the nostril wide,
> Hold hard the breath and bend up every spirit
> To his full height! On, on you noblest English . . .
> I see you stand like greyhounds in the slips,
> Straining upon the start. The game's afoot!
> Follow your spirit, and upon this charge
> Cry "God for Harry, England, and Saint George!"

King Henry, *Henry V.* 3, 1

Take-Away Ideas

* A good team can add much to communication success.
* Choose team makeup to blend talents well.
* Everybody has to pull together for a good team to work.
* Adjust team makeup if it's not working.
* Now march unto the breach as a winning team!

Chapter 20

❧❀❦

The Readiness Is All: Prepare Well

The readiness is all.

Hamlet, Hamlet. 5, 2

Ask almost any successful communicator—speaker, meeting chair, negotiator—for one tip on success, and the answer is likely to be "preparation." In principle, most of us subscribe to this. In practice, pressures and procrastination result in last-minute preparation, skipped rehearsals, and arrangements based on chance. Readiness may not be "all," but it is "a lot" when it comes to making a professional and successful impression.

While care in preparation concerns many facets of communication, it especially applies when you're using media—audiovisual gear, public address systems, and electronic vehicles.

Rehearse Your Parts

Come, sit down, every mother's son and rehearse your parts.

Quince, A Midsummer Night's Dream. 3, 1

The value of practice is often downplayed. "Don't need it; I've done this many times." "Don't have time, got other priorities." Here's a clue: Those who say such things are likely those who need practice the most. The excellent communicators often are the most receptive to practice and coaching, perhaps because they've seen how important it has been to their success. In this camp are presidential candidates who simulate debates ahead of the real thing, attorneys who conduct mock trials, and presentation teams going after big money. Even superstar athletes like Tiger Woods and Venus Williams are constantly going back to the practice range to iron out (or stroke out) even the tiny flaws.

In coaching many individuals or teams for important engagements—proposal presentations, job interviews, court testimonies—I've found that an essential part of preparation is the rehearsal—and often a second or third one. With some helpful feedback the improvement is often significant. Which is better: to have your flaws and warts surface first in a private session with a coach or colleague, or wait for them to appear—as they will—in front of the real audience?

> We will meet; and there we may rehearse most
>   obscenely and courageously. Take pains; be perfect:
>   adieu.
>
> Bottom, *A Midsummer Night's Dream.* 1, 2

I recall one sales chap who resisted rehearsal, with the philosophy "I don't want to come across too slick. I prefer to wing it." That approach got him by for a while, until he bombed out on an important customer encounter. The customer said he was not likely to buy from someone who didn't value his time enough to show up prepared.

Get Help from Your Wise Friends

Make choice of whom your wisest friends you will,
And they shall hear and judge 'twixt you and me.

King Claudius, *Hamlet.* 4, 5

Practicing alone may help you smooth out the flow of your message. Rehearsing before a mirror can show you how you will look to others. Having the dog as receiver can remind you to engage your audience, though that audience might not engage back.

"Practice makes perfect" is the old recommendation, except it's only partly true. Practice your golf swing every day, and you'll see *some* improvement. Get some helpful feedback from a coach, and you may see *significant* improvement as she spots the ineffective techniques you're merely repeating. Shaquille O'Neal is a great basketball player and a lousy free throw shooter. Yet he practices diligently. A coach observed, "Yes he practices a lot, but he practices poor technique."

For some situations, such as job interviews, training sessions, or presentations, you'll find practice more realistic and productive if you call on colleagues to sit in and give you feedback. This is especially valuable for people taking on new roles, such as content experts conducting training sessions, new employee orientations, and proposal presentations.

For many high-stakes communications, companies assign special review "pink" and "red" teams whose role is to review written proposals or oral presentations, assess them in great detail, and then offer feedback aimed at making them better, which it almost always does.

Videotaping and review has proven beneficial for evaluating many oral situations: training simulations and role plays, customer interactions, media appearances, supervisor-subordinate counseling, and more. With video allowing you to see for yourself how good or bad you are, it's hard to deny the results revealed. An associate may point out, "You have a bad habit of saying 'y' know' a lot." You may deny it until you see the video and find out (1) you do have a problem, (2) it's a serious distraction, and (3) you're well advised to fix it.

Put Your Helpful Critics To 't

> O gentle lady, do not put me to 't;
> For I am nothing, if not critical.
>
> Iago, *Othello*. 2, 1

It's important to get the right sort of person to be a reviewer. Some people are reluctant to play the critic role, following the biblical adage "Thou shalt not judge." A reviewer whose standard comment is "That was wonderful; don't change anything" is not helping the team much (unless it really is fault-free, which is not likely). A hypercritical person or one lacking tact may not be a good choice either, because we tend to reject overly harsh or insensitive feedback.

> Forbear to judge, for we are sinners all.
> Close up his eyes and draw the curtain close;
> And let us all to meditation.
>
> Henry, *Henry VI, Part 2*. 3, 3

If you're assigned the reviewer role, take the responsibility seriously. Good reviewers have several attributes:

* They know enough about the subject to make enlightened assessments.

* They can identify specific strengths and weaknesses in both content and communication technique.

* They are astute enough to help you with fixes.

* They have the right combination of tact and assertiveness to give feedback in a manner such that it will be received, digested, and acted upon.

> When you are hearing a matter between party and
>   party, if you chance to be pinched with the colic,
>   you make faces like mummers.
>
> Menenius, Coriolanus. 2, 1

Don't let your listener/reviewer style taint the sender's communication. If you listen with a scowl, puzzled demeanor, or happy-go-lucky manner, this can change the sender's communication. The best results seem to come if reviewers play their parts much as the real receivers would.

To "Amend the Faults," Balance Feedback

> You must needs learn, lord to amend this fault:
> Though sometimes it show greatness, courage, blood—
> And that's the dearest grace it renders you—
> Yet sometimes it doth present harsh rage,
> Defect of manners, want of government,
> Pride, haughtiness, opinion and disdain.
>
> Worcester, Henry IV, Part 1. 3, 1

In coaching sessions, I've seen the value of providing balanced feedback. If you point out only the negatives, the receiver can get frustrated: "Didn't I do anything right?" You can often see the resentment appear and then rise as the forehead flushes, the temples start to throb, the mouth curls down, and the attitude shifts from receptive to defensive: "All, right, Mr. Big Shot, let me tell you a few things *you* did wrong in our meeting last week!" As a reviewer, make the effort to identify several positive attributes before commenting on the defects.

> My Lord Sebastian,
> The truth you speak doth lack some gentleness,
> And time to speak it in: you rub the sore,
> When you should bring the plaster.
>
> Gonzalo, *The Tempest*. 2, 1

Abrasiveness may work in the short term, but it can damage the receiver's self-esteem and build long-term resentment (read *revenge*). Skillful feedback given in a tactful manner helps the immediate situation and builds the relationship. Effective reviewers go beyond just flagging deficiencies; they suggest possible ways to correct them. A good coach doesn't just say what you did wrong; he offers constructive advice about how to do it better.

Take Feedback Seriously

> So again, good night.
> I must be cruel, only to be kind:
> Thus bad begins, and worse remains behind.
>
> Hamlet, *Hamlet*. 3, 4

> You are dull, Casca.
>
> Cassius, *Julius Caesar*. 1, 3

Did anyone ever tell you that you were a lousy communicator? Or suggest that you'd be more successful if only you'd fix certain behaviors? "You're so grumpy." "Why are you so defensive?" "Don't talk with your mouth full." A common tendency is to immediately reject such well-meaning (sometimes) and valuable (sometimes) feedback.

> Better a little chiding than a great deal of heart-break.
>
> Mistress Page, *The Merry Wives of Windsor*. 5, 3

When receiving feedback, listen to it (shut mouth and activate ears). If you are perceived as reacting strongly to feedback or you go on the attack, this can cause reviewers to either become equally aggressive, leading to nonproductive conflict, or go into protective mode, decline to continue, and stifle valuable feedback.

Arrive on Time, If Not Three Hours Too Soon

> Better three hours too soon than a minute too late.
>
> Ford, *The Merry Wives of Windsor*. 2, 2

Many marketing managers have become firm believers in this axiom, some the hard way. Requests for proposals (RFPs) often provide a drop-dead due date and time for proposals. Work diligently for three months on a proposal, spending a million dollars. Then show up a minute late and the customer won't accept it. A very painful experience as those who've experienced it will attest.

When getting ready for a meeting or presentation, get there well ahead of time. That way you can round up that projector that was promised, was there yesterday, but isn't there now.

I will knog your urinals about your knave's coxcomb
for missing your meetings and appointments.

Evans, *The Merry Wives of Windsor.* 3, 1

Few things convey the impression of lack of professionalism more than your arriving late, not being ready, or neglecting to check the facility when it was your responsibility. Meeting productivity is immediately affected as well if progress has to be held up while you or a swiftly assigned gofer heads off to locate the missing bulb. Those kept waiting by your performance may not be pleased, and, who knows, may even knog your urinals. Ever had that happen to you?

A complicating factor is when the meeting is held away from your own facility, such as the customer's shop across town, or even in Los Angeles and you work in Chicago. Put plenty of extra contingency time into your schedule so you can relax (a relative term) en route instead of frantically trying to catch up.

The Los Angeles MTA (Metropolitan Transit Authority) Board found out that ignoring promptness pays a price, "Angry members of the Bus Riders Union walked out of a public hearing Saturday after no one on the MTA board initially showed up to hear the concerns of hundreds of people about plans. . . .

"To cheers and applause, Bus Riders Union activist Cirilo Juarez announced that more than 100 members of the group would leave the hearing . . .

" 'We are wasting our time,' Juarez said, 'This is very, very . . . disrespectful.' "

Take-Away Ideas

* Readiness may not be all, but it can be vital.
* Make reviews an integral part of your communication plan.
* Get good reviewers and listen to their feedback.
* Meet your commitments.
* Be on time, if not well ahead of schedule.

Chapter 21

Unveil That Knave!
This Is a Competition

He has not so much brain as ear-wax.

Thersites, *Troilus and Cressida*. 5, 1

Now let's look at how to handle your competitors. In the world of business there often is someone who wants your job. Or you may be in a competition for internal dollars to pursue a favorite research project or buy a new computer. The decision makers may not know your competitor as well as you do, so it's useful to have a few choice expressions in your toolkit, which at opportune times you can draw from to capture the essence of the other candidate.

Go Ahead—Blow the Whistle

A slippery and subtle knave.

Iago, *Othello*. 2, 1

Actually, not *just* a knave but . . .

A whoreson beetle-headed, flap-ear'd knave!

> Petruchio, *Taming of the Shrew*. 4, 1

Why not go for broke and reveal the full story about this upstart?

> A knave; a rascal; an eater of broken meats; a base,
> proud, shallow, beggary, three-suited, hundred-
> pound, filthy, worsted-stocking knave; a lily-livered,
> action-taking knave; a whoreson, glass gazing,
> superserviceable, finical rogue; one-trunk-inheriting
> slave; one that wouldst be a bawd in way of good
> service, and art nothing but the composition of a
> knave, beggar, coward, pandar, and the son and heir
> of a mongrel bitch.

> Kent, *King Lear*. 2, 2

Then again, it may not be just one scoundrel who's after your job or who thinks his mousetrap is better than yours, it's often a whole team. When the stakes are high, the size of the competition often is increased. You've got to be ready to alert key decision makers about what a sorry bunch they are and what a mistake they'd be making to go for their proposition over yours.

> O villains, vipers, damn'd without redemption!
> Dogs, easily won to fawn on any man!
> Snakes, in my heart-blood warm'd, that sting my heart.

> Richard, *Richard II*. 3, 2

Wow! Richard is referring to the guys who are about to dethrone him. This looks like a truly rough bunch to go up against. Wouldn't you much rather have these sinister characters on your own team? Reconsider your strategy: Abandon plan A and enact plan B, with your new team made up of vipers, dogs, and snakes.

Going After Brand X

> O, if men were to be saved by merit, what hole in hell
> were hot enough for him? This is the most
> omnipotent villain that ever cried "Stand!" to a true
> man.
>
> Falstaff, *Henry IV, Part 1*. 1, 2

You know it—our opponent is as villainous as Falstaff's nemesis, Poins—but do the decision makers know it? This is not the time to be timid. I made that mistake not once but twice when running for public office. My strategy was to stick to the high ground, run a positive campaign, and say nothing derogatory about my two opponents. They both had serious skeletons in their respective closets, both were clearly unqualified compared with me, and, if I recall correctly, they even smoked cigars. But did I mention any of these juicy tidbits to the voting populace? Of course not. Did I win? Of course not.

> [He is] a gentleman that loves to hear himself talk, and
> will speak more in a minute than he will stand to in
> a month.
>
> Romeo, *Romeo and Juliet*. 2, 4

Another candidate chose a different tactic from the course I followed, with loud and clear proclamations about the true nature of his opponent. In the Florida race for the U.S. Senate in 1952, George Smathers had these harsh words to say about his opponent, Claude Pepper: "Are you aware that the candidate is known all over Washington as a shameless extrovert? Not only that, but this man is reliably reported to have practiced nepotism with his sister-in-law and he has a sister who was once a wicked thespian in New York. He matriculated with co-eds at the University, and it is an established fact that before his marriage he habitually practiced celibacy." Smathers won. Why didn't I follow his proven path to success?

> . . . elvish-mark'd, abortive, rooting hog!
>
> Margaret, *Richard III*. 1, 3

Here the widow of the former king, with a reasonable degree of pique, is unloading on Richard III. If you want to know the real story about Richard, just ask Margaret—or, it appears, you don't even need to ask. Her stated opinion may be perhaps a bit unfair in referring to his physical characteristics.

Want Some Help in Epithet-Honing?

> O thou well-skill'd in curses, stay awhile,
> And teach me how to curse mine enemies.
>
> Queen Elizabeth, *Richard III*. 4, 4

A good teacher is always of value. Here may be another role for a colleague with specialized linguistic skills or even a devious external coach.

Here are a few starters; you check the desired box and fill in the appropriate name:

My competitor, ☐ Mr. ☐ Ms. ☐ It _____:

☐ "the bastard, whose spirits toil in frame of villainies"

> Benedick, *Much Ado About Nothing*. 4, 1

☐ "[whose brain] is as dry as the remainder biscuit after a voyage"

> Jaques, *As You Like It*. 2, 7

☐ "a hungry lean-faced villain, a mere anatomy"

> Antipholus E., *The Comedy of Errors*. 5, 1

☐ "a most notable coward, an infinite and endless liar"

Lord, *All's Well That Ends Well.* 3, 6

The entire Brand X team:

☐ "Asses, fools, dolts! Chaff and bran"

Pandarus, *Troilus and Cressida.* 1, 2

☐ "smiling, smooth, detested parasites"

Timon, *Timon of Athens.* 3, 6

☐ "true-bred cowards as ever turned back"

Poins, *Henry IV, Part 1.* 1, 2

☐ "apes of idleness"

King Henry, *Henry IV, Part 2.* 4, 5

(These also may have application to ☐ IRS auditors, ☐ Congress, ☐ Upper management, ☐ Your team's coaching staff, ☐ ———)

In modern times we have few good practitioners to learn from, though Churchill, Harry Truman, George Wallace, Muhammed Ali, and Joan Rivers have done some good work. For true creativity and inspiration, look to the older masters who polished these skills to a high sheen:

* Mark Twain: "Reader, suppose you were an idiot; and suppose you were a member of Congress; but I repeat myself."

Nancy McPhee, *The Book of Insults*

* Benjamin Disraeli: "If a traveler were informed that such a man was the Leader of the House of Commons, he might begin to comprehend how the Egyptians worshiped an insect."

The Book of Insults

* Teddy Roosevelt: "A cold-blooded, narrow-minded, obstinate, timid old psalm-singing politician." And he was talking about a member of his own party.

David Olive, *Political Babble*

* H. L. Mencken: "The American people, taking one with another, constitute the most timorous, sniveling, poltroonish, ignominious mob of serfs and goose-steppers ever gathered under one flag since the end of the Middle Ages."

Prejudices: A Selection

* Susan, in her famous speech on the final night of *Survivor*—a masterful performance slicing up the other female finalist.

If you're still having trouble coming up with a good epithet or the truly appropriate description of that unworthy scoundrel who wants your job, here's a handy tool: The Bard's Invective Generator. This is borrowed from Philip Broughton's "Systematic Buzz Phrase Projector," a three-column system for coming up with a high-sounding, suitably innocuous buzz phrase, such as "parallel reciprocal contingency." From the Internet, a comprehensive three-column system is contained in *Create Your Own Shakespearean Insults* by Jerry Maguire (*www. in-machina.com/~reece/humor/shakespeare-insults*).

Here you just pick three numbers or select a word from each column to develop your very own tailored epithet, suitable for hurling. Thus if you pick 349, you will get "fawning logger-headed puttock." Don't you know one of these? (These also may help you more precisely focus your opinion of your own boss or that new efficiency expert the department just brought in—or is he more a bulls-pizzle?)

Column 1	Column 2	Column 3
1. boil-brained	1. odoriferous	1. bulls-pizzle
2. decayed	2. droning	2. lump

3. fawning	3. tickle-brained	3. sot
4. stale	4. logger-headed	4. gudgeon
5. malignant	5. gorbellied	5. carbuncle
6. prating	6. knotty-pated	6. lout
7. lumpish	7. stony-hearted	7. maggot-pie
8. mammering	8. ill-faced	8. stench
9. sneaking	9. clay-brained	9. puttock
10. lean-witted	10. toad-spotted	10. scut

Now, if you're still a bit timid about applying the clear-cut wisdom contained in this chapter, possibly even questioning the ethics of such behavior, just recall these words from the witches in Macbeth:

"Fair is foul, and foul is fair." So if you still hold back, there's little hope for you, you 892.

The Coup de Grace

Now let's consider some genuinely serious strategy to take Brand X out of the competition. Your concept is clearly superior, but those decision makers are waffling, and perhaps even leaning the wrong way (probably due to some underhanded tactics on the part of the competition). You want some insurance to gain that extra edge. What better than to have Brand X drop out of the race? Here's the plan. Before the critical meeting, in which all sides will have some time to state their case, convince the meeting manager to insert in the script after Brand X's moment, these stage directions (from *The Winter's Tale*, 3, 3), which have delighted Shakespeare aficionados across the centuries:

(Exit, pursued by a bear.)

To have this successfully executed, you will of course have to include one bear, hungry, in your budget.

Take-Away Ideas

* Decision makers may value your insights about competitors.

* Be ready to expose the competition as the incompetents and scoundrels they are.

* When revealing the true story about Brand X, cast timidity aside.

* For descriptive language about competitors, call on the Bard, a true master.

Chapter 22

A Hit, a Very Palpable Hit! You Won!

> O such a day,
> So fought, so follow'd, and so fairly won,
> Came not till now to dignify the times,
> Since Caesar's fortunes!
>
> Lord Bardolph, *Henry IV, Part 2.* 1, 1

Good work. Your proposition has been accepted. You passed the test. Your client was found innocent. Your team won a tough competition and a big contract. Or, maybe they weren't overwhelmed by your arguments, went to sleep during your presentation, and—horrors—chose Brand X over you. It's time to reap the rewards, and communicate appropriately.

Well Ended: Fine Words Indeed

> This business is well ended.
>
> Polonius, *Hamlet.* 2, 2

> A hit, a very palpable hit.
>
> Osric, *Hamlet.* 5, 2

You've carried the day; your story was a clear hit, apparently. But to be certain you got the right word, keep this line handy:

> Tell me if you speak in jest or no.
>
> Lady Percy, *Henry IV, Part 1.* 2, 3

This is to suggest a word of caution about getting too carried away with your celebration. Sometimes people pop the champagne cork too soon, thinking they won, only to discover later they really didn't. That is painful. A classic example was the presidential election in 1948. Thomas Dewey, the Republican governor of New York, was expected to easily defeat the Democratic nominee and incumbent president, Harry Truman. A famous photo shows a grinning Truman holding up a newspaper with the headline blaring "Dewey Defeats Truman!"

The quote of Bardolph's glee at the opening of this chapter falls in that category. His jubilation had a short life, as he had received bad information, and his side hadn't won at all. So you want to be sure you got the right information.

It's Thank-You Time

> I am so attired in wonder,
> I know not what to say.
>
> Benedick, *Much Ado About Nothing.* 4, 1

Now, assuming your cause actually did win out, it's always a good idea to extend your appreciation to the wise individual or committee that reviewed your proposition and gave it the thumbs-up.

> For this relief much thanks.
>
> Francisco, *Hamlet.* 1, 1

Since you and your team have been hanging on tenterhooks, desperately waiting for a positive result, your physical and mental health still in jeopardy, your marriage finally patching up, this favorable decision ends a long period of uncertainty, hope, and fervent prayers.

Perhaps even suck up to them a bit. There's more opportunity ahead, so lay some groundwork.

> You are a worthy judge;
> You know the law, your exposition
> Hath been most sound.
>
> Shylock, *The Merchant of Venice*. 4, 1

Good Fellowship All Around

> O brave new world,
> That has such people in't!
>
> Miranda, *The Tempest*. 5, 1

With your success, a pat on the back for good work done and recognized is in order. If yours was a solo effort, treat yourself to at least a night out. If it was a team effort, thank your colleagues for their good services.

> We are such stuff
> As dreams are made on.
>
> Prospero, *The Tempest*. 4, 1

Want some good words to compliment your leader, say the project head who led your team to a positive conclusion?

> . . . a gentleman of excellent breeding, admirable
> discourse, of great admittance, authentic in your

place and person, generally allowed for your many
warlike, court-like, and learned preparations.

Ford, *The Merry Wives of Windsor*. 2, 2

Lay it on (there may be opportunity here for the better slots on the
newly won program; after all, Ford was lying here as he flattered
Falstaff, the recipient of this praise).

Pray heavens he be;
For I have served him, and the man commands
Like a full soldier.

Montano, *Othello*. 2, 1

Since the world of business consists of people with a variety of leaders, with a variety of techniques in their repertoire, and with a range
of ethical approaches, you might want to put a more specific flavor
to the praise you extend your own winning team leader.

Thou art the best o' th' cut-throats.

Macbeth, *Macbeth*. 3, 4

Is that high praise or what?

It's Party Time!

Come in, and let us banquet royally,
After this golden day of victory.

King Charles, *Henry VI, Part 1*. 1, 6

Don't forget the victory party. This is a good opportunity to cheer
together, to bask in the glory of a hard-fought and successful effort.
Sometimes leaders skip this important occasion and continue right

on to the next activity. On many tasks, people have put in long hours—usually unpaid—cut short family activities, and endured considerable stress. It's time to celebrate!

> Well,
> To the latter end of a fray, and the beginning of a feast
> Fits a dull fighter and a keen guest.
>
> Falstaff, *Henry IV, Part 1*. 4, 2

The pursuit of success for many communication projects entails a lot of hard work. Serving on a special task force or a proposal team may involve dozens of people and extend over weeks, with much pressure.

> And now what rests but that we spend the time
> With stately triumphs, mirthful comic shows,
> Such as befits the pleasure of the Court?
>
> King Edward, *Henry VI, Part 3*. 5, 7

> There's not a minute of our lives should stretch
> Without some pleasure now.
>
> Antony, *Antony and Cleopatra*. 1, 1

Time to Catch Up on the ZZZZZs

> Enjoy the honey-heavy dew of slumber:
> Thou hast no figures nor no fantasies,
> Which busy care draws in the brains of men;
> Therefore thou sleep'st so sound.
>
> Brutus, *Julius Caesar*. 2, 1

To sleep: perchance to dream.

Hamlet, Hamlet. 3, 1

Remember all that sleep you lost, because of either an overactive brain or heavy anxiety about what you had to do? Now you might actually catch up.

O sleep, O gentle sleep,
Nature's soft nurse.

Henry, Henry IV, Part 2. 3, 1

Sleep that knits up the ravell'd sleave of care,
The death of each day's life, sore labour's bath,
Balm of hurt minds, great nature's second course,
Chief nourisher in life's feast.

Macbeth, Macbeth. 2, 2

Take-Away Ideas

* When you've won, celebrate and wind down.
* Spread thank-yous around liberally.
* Restore your health and relationships.

Chapter 23

———⊰⟡⊱———

Done to Death by Slanderous Tongues! Uh Oh, You Lost

Flat burglary as ever was committed.

Dogberry, Much Ado About Nothing. 4, 2

Sometimes your best efforts come up short. The boss didn't buy it and sent you back to the drawing board, you failed to get the nod for the promotion, or the review committee gave the business to the other team. You still have some communication needs to be met. Let's examine a few.

First, Let the Steam Blow!

O heavy ignorance! that praisest the worst best.

Desdemona, Othello. 2, 1

You may take the loss well, or, then again, some severe reaction may be in order.

O, horrible! O, horrible! Most horrible!

Ghost, Hamlet. 1, 5

Perhaps you choose to lament that the judgment smacks of favoritism, politics, underhandedness, or the day's horoscope. Or even dirty tricks on the part of the competition.

> Done to death by slanderous tongues.
>
> Claudio, *Much Ado About Nothing*. 5, 3

You know well that it was a bunch of gutless, low-level, bought-off ignoramuses who made this bum decision that cost you that plum win (and perhaps your plum job). But what can one do?

> O that I were a god, to shoot forth thunder
> Upon these paltry, servile, abject drudges!
>
> Suffolk, *Henry VI, Part 2*. 4, 1

Now that you've considered the various options, and rejected the impractical ones, maybe it's time at least to commiserate together.

Time to Lick the Wounds

> Come,
> Let's have one other gaudy night: call to me
> All my sad captains; fill our bowls once more;
> Let's mock the midnight bell.
>
> Antony (before his death), *Antony and Cleopatra*. 3, 13

It's not nearly so much fun when you come in second, or third, or last. Still, there's value in bringing the team together again, for appreciation and mutual reassurance.

> I see this is the time that the unjust man doth thrive.
>
> Autoclytus, *The Winter's Tale*. 4, 4

While you're crying in your margaritas, you'll feel better if you remind yourself that it wasn't your ineptness but mankind's low standards that have done you in.

Let It Go: Moan and Groan

> Let us seek out some desolate shade, and there
> Weep our sad bosoms empty.
>
> Malcolm, *Macbeth*. 4, 3

It was your baby. You thought you had a sound story, but you were wrong. Not only did your cause go down, but your very career may be in shambles.

> Let's shake our heads, and say . . .
> "We have seen better days."
>
> Flavius, *Timon of Athens*. 4, 2

This may call for some suitable self-flagellation, such as gnashing of teeth, rending of clothes, pouring ashes on head, banging head on wall . . . So why not engage in a bit of much-deserved self-pity?

> When, in disgrace with fortune and men's eyes,
> I all alone beweep my outcast state,
> And trouble deaf heaven with my bootless cries,
> And look upon myself, and curse my fate,
> Wishing me like to one more rich in hope,
> Featured like him, like him with friends possess'd,
> Desiring this man's art and that man's scope,
> With what I most enjoy contented least;
>
> *Sonnet 29*

In the words so well phrased by Peggy Lee, "Is that all there is?"

You're on a Roll—Don't Quit So Soon

Whip me, ye devils . . .
Blow me about in winds! Roast me in sulfur!
Wash me in steep-down gulfs of liquid fire!

Othello, Othello. 5, 2

I have touch'd the highest point of all my greatness;
And, from that full meridian of my glory,
I haste now to my setting. I shall fall
Like a bright exhalation in the evening,
And no man see me more.

Cardinal Wolsey, Henry VIII. 3, 2

For centuries in Japan, leaders who perceive themselves as having failed the team or country, if they are honorable men, have taken sword in hand and committed hari-kari. This never caught on outside Japan.

Still, there may be leaders or team members with a failed cause who might find satisfaction in high-intensity moaning and groaning. If that is not regarded as adequate self-abuse, they may appreciate knowing of the remedy sought by the Earl of Gloucester, once high and mighty but now heavily out of favor (if you call being blinded, totally destroyed in position and finances, and thrown into the wilderness out of favor):

There is a cliff whose high and bending head
Looks fearfully in the confined deep.
Bring me but to the very brim of it,

And I'll repair the misery thou dost bear
With something rich about me: from that place
I shall no leading need.

Gloucester, King Lear. 4, 1

Leading, of course, to the appropriate benediction:

Close up his eyes and draw the curtain close;
And let us all to meditation.

Henry, Henry VI, Part 2. 3, 3

But who has the last laugh?

See how the pangs of death do make him grin!

Warwick, Henry VI, Part 2. 3, 3

Time to Pay the Piper

You must prepare your bosom for his knife.

Portia, The Merchant of Venice. 4, 1

It turns out upper management is not pleased about your losing effort, valiant though it was. Hard as it is to believe, they may actually blame *you*. So be prepared if they come out with such expressions as . . .

The complaints I hear of thee are grievous.

Prince, Henry IV, Part 1. 2, 4

The ringleader and head of all this rout.

Buckingham, Henry VI, Part 2. 2, 1

Off with his head!

Richard, Richard III. 3, 4

Finger-Pointing Option 1: The Team Was a Bunch of Losers

Company, villainous company, hath been the spoil of
me.

Falstaff, Henry IV, Part 1. 3, 3

On the other hand as the top marketeer, you know that you certainly were not to blame for this terrible defeat. It clearly was the fault of the sad lot you were saddled with.

I am betray'd by keeping company
With men like you, men of inconstancy.

Biron, Love's Labour's Lost. 4, 3

Your leadership was obviously of the highest rank. You know this because you have a master's degree and a certificate from the Effective Leadership Seminar, and you took only thirty minutes to digest the principles from *The One-Minute Manager*. But the company gave you a bunch of misfits to work with.

. . . general louts . . .

Volumnia, Coriolanus. 3, 2

Finger-Pointing Option 2: It Was the Boss's Fault

Sir, you may thank yourself for this great loss.

Sebastian, The Tempest. 2, 1

From the other perspective, as one of the "louts," you know where the blame lies. You and your colleagues gave it your all, in spite of weak leadership from the top. You knew right from the start that this project was headed for disaster, and all your keen ideas fell on deaf ears. You all kept plugging, realizing it was probably going to be an effort in vain. Sure enough, it was, and you know exactly why.

> How many fruitless pranks this ruffian hath botch'd up.
>
> Olivia, *Twelfth Night.* 4, 1

So let the boss have it! Call a spade a spade! Put the cards on the table! Vent your spleen!

> That reverend vice, that grey iniquity, that father ruffian . . .
>
> Prince, *Henry IV, Part 1.* 2, 4

Actually, I don't advocate this confrontational approach unless (1) you're nearing retirement with a good pension, 401(k) plan, or vast.com stock options ripe for cashing in; (2) you have six outstanding job offers waiting; or (3) you've decided on a major lifestyle change and already have your tickets for a three-year retreat with a guru in Bhutan.

Finger-Pointing Option 3: Politics, Favoritism, Dirty Tricks

> There's a knot, a ging, a pack, a conspiracy against me.
>
> Ford, *The Merry Wives of Windsor.* 4, 2

Regardless of where the blame lies, you lost. One proven way to feel better is to vent your spleen against the judges and jury. After all, what do they know anyway? It's sad to think that your fortune rests with such incompetents. Oops—enough, let's let the Bard have a go at them.

> The carping censures of the world.
>
> Gloucester, Richard III. 3, 5

> Abusing better men than they can ever be . . .
>
> Lovell, Henry VIII. 1, 3

> The plague of Greece upon thee, thou mongrel beef-witted lord!
>
> Thersites, Troilus and Cressida. 2, 1

Now, doesn't that feel better? Nothing like a little spleen venting to mitigate unwarranted maltreatment.

OK, Back to Work

> I come to thee for charitable license,
> That we may wander o'er this bloody field
> To book our dead, and then to bury them.
>
> Montjoy, Henry V. 4, 7

Are you over it now? Has the weeping and wailing phase passed? Then it's time to leave the negativism behind and move forward to the next challenge—slightly bruised but undoubtedly wiser, with some useful lessons learned.

> Be cheerful; wipe thine eyes:
> Some falls are means the happier to arise.
>
> Lucius, Cymbeline. 4, 2

Often a setback contains the elements for success the next time. By reviewing the processes and decisions for the previous effort, valuable lessons can be derived that may be applied to the next campaign.

Take-Away Ideas

* When you lose, explore all options for feeling better (or worse, if you prefer).

* Place the blame where it clearly belongs—with someone else.

* Tally the lessons learned and move back into the fray, bruised but wiser.

Part VII

Continuing Onward

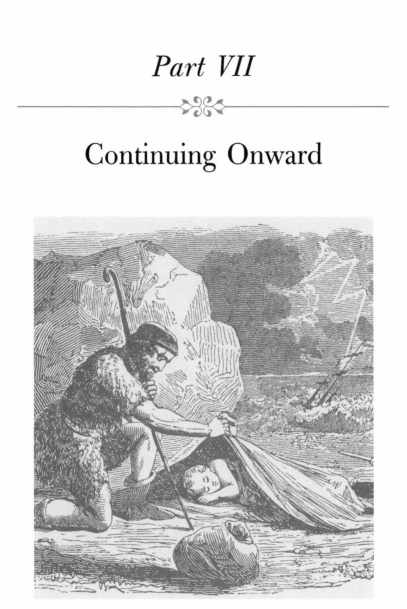

The Winter's Tale. 3, 3

You're in the home stretch. All the hard work is done. All the insights from the Bard, and perhaps a few others, have been perused. All that remains is to start applying them to your own world of work, family, friends, affiliations, and causes. It's time to start achieving swift and clear benefits: better results, improved relationships, more fun (with the Bard as guide), career advancement, enhanced self-esteem, and maybe solving the world's problems.

Chapter 24

Speak—It's Your Cue: Moving Forward

Let us every one go home
And laugh this sport o'er a country fire.

Mrs. Page, The Merry Wives of Windsor. 5, 5

We're almost through with this endeavor of linking the four-centuries-old words of Shakespeare and his spectrum of characters to our contemporary business world. As you've read these chapters, I trust you've been applying them to your working world, and beyond. Perhaps you've found that some of these quotes, actions, or descriptions to fit surprisingly well to your own communication with others, certainly with your bosses, probably with your colleagues and customers, and maybe even with your friends and family.

If you've taken the Bard's advice to heart and seriously applied his tips, you've undoubtedly seen some positive results. Your customers, colleagues, and even the boss have been commenting about how you've become a much better communicator. Now build on that success and continue adding to your power and the rewards that follow.

I would applaud thee to the very echo,
That should applaud again.

Macbeth, Macbeth. 5, 3

If the Bard's insights have led you to measurably enhance your communication skills, others cannot have failed to notice and may have even commented that you have become a person . . .

> . . . whose words all ears took captive.
>
> Lafeu, All's Well That Ends Well. 5, 3

If you've made it this far, you have shown a high degree of dedication (or are determined to find a useful kernel even if it doesn't appear until the final chapter). So let me and one of my favorite Shakespearean figures of full stature in physique and wit offer you a toast of appreciation and success:

> God give thee the spirit of persuasion and him the ears
> of profiting, that what thou speakest may move and
> what he hears may be believed.
>
> Falstaff, Henry IV, Part 1. 1, 2

Resist not the challenges that this book may present you, and the potential rewards that you may receive by applying the principles. These recharged skills may open new doors for you as you advance toward your career and personal goals. Heed these words being pondered by another character, this one on the pompous side, as he reads from a departmental memo:

> Be not afraid of greatness: some are born great, some
> achieve greatness, and some have greatness thrust
> upon 'em.
>
> Malvolio, Twelfth Night. 2, 5

Why not you?

Are You Inspired?

Recall from Chapter 13 that King Henry V gathered information from his troops by wandering around in the middle of the night. The next day he spoke to his vastly outnumbered troops before the big battle. This occurred on a day of significance to the troops, St. Crispin's Day.

> This day is call'd the feast of Crispian.
> He that outlives this day, and comes safe home,
> Will stand a-tip-toe when the day is named,
> And rouse him at the name of Crispian.
> He that shall live this day, and see old age,
> Will yearly on the vigil feast his neighbours,
> And say "To-morrow is Saint Crispian."
> Then will he strip his sleeve and show his scars,
> And say "These wounds I had on Crispin's day."
> Old men forget: yet all shall be forgot,
> But he'll remember with advantages
> What feats he did that day: then shall our names,
> Familiar in his mouth as household words,
> Harry the king, Bedford and Exeter,
> Warwick and Talbot, Salisbury and Gloucester,
> Be in their flowing cups freshly remember'd.
> This story shall the good man teach his son;
> And Crispin Crispian shall ne'er go by,
> From this day to the ending of the world,
> But we in it shall be remembered;
> We few, we happy few, we band of brothers;
> For he to-day that sheds his blood with me
> Shall be my brother; be he ne'er so vile,
> This day shall gentle his condition:

And gentlemen in England now a-bed
Shall think themselves accursed they were not here,
And hold their manhoods cheap whiles any speaks
That fought with us upon Saint Crispin's day.

King Henry, Henry V. 4. 3

If you read this aloud, you may feel an irresistible urge to head off for the recruiting office. This is regarded by many as one of the most powerful communications in the entire Shakespeare repertoire. Oh yes, the outcome was a huge upset win for Henry's troops.

Let me leave you with some of the major messages this book has been conveying:

* Good professional expertise *and* communication capability makes a powerhouse combination.

* Many good people are marginal communicators, thus limiting their effectiveness and career opportunities.

* You can become a proficient communicator with commitment and attention to the many facets involved: sender, receiver, message, medium, feedback.

* Take inspiration from these words of the Bard and start going on your own campaign to become a better communicator, and reap the rewards.

* Remember, if you decline the opportunity, your competitor may not.

Speak Count, 'tis your cue.

Beatrice, Much Ado About Nothing. 2, 1

Go for it.

Credits

Chapter 1

p. 8: . . . *a bad job at them.*" "When Speech, Um, Gets in the Way of, Ah, Getting Ahead," *Washington Post*, 8/20/00, p. L1.

Chapter 2

p. 14: . . . *frictions and competitions.*" Marlin Fitzwater, *Call the Briefing* (Holbrook, MA: Adams Media Corp., 1995), p. 75.

p. 16: . . . *belittling employees in front of others.*" Bruce Nash and Allan Zullo, *The Mis-Fortune 500* (New York: Pocket Books, 1988).

p. 17: . . . *defenders grew smaller.*" Fitzwater, *Call the Briefing*, p. 75.

p. 18: . . . *The intensity of communications is unmistakable.*" Tom Peters and Robert Waterman, *In Search of Excellence: Lessons from America's Best-Run Companies* (New York: Harper & Row, 1988), p. 122.

p. 21: . . . *they can sabotage anything.*" Neil Morgan, "Dreaming Big: Could Our City Become Model in Leadership?" *San Diego Union-Tribune*, 9/28/00, p. 3.

Chapter 3

p. 32: . . . *have a good product and market yourself.*" Interview with Sharan Wendel, Benbow, CA, 8/25/00.

Chapter 4

p. 38: . . . *to follow the voice of James Earl Jones.*" "2000 Sydney Olympics Opening Ceremony," NBC-TV, 8/15/00.

p. 41: . . . *very fast talkers and monotonous voices. Wall Street Journal*, 11/5/93.

p. 42: . . . *Director's legendary mumbling.*" Bob Woodward, *Veil: The Secret Wars of the CIA* (New York: Simon & Schuster, 1987).

p. 42: . . . *Go figure. PBS*, 9/8/00.

Chapter 5

p. 50: . . . *the Spartan response was "If."* Michael Macrone, *Brush Up Your Classics* (New York: Gramercy Press, 1999), p. 34.

p. 53: . . . *no one caught the significance."* Fitzwater, *Call the Briefing*, p. 209 [emphasis added].

p. 55: . . . *the beer with the silent P."* Nash and Zullo, *The Mis-Fortune 500*, p. 91.

p. 56: . . . *catch them doing something right."* Ken Blanchard, *The One Minute Manager* (San Diego: Blanchard Training and Development, 1982).

p. 57: . . . *their answer was 13 percent.* Rensis Likert, *New Patterns of Management* (New York: McGraw-Hill, 1961).

p. 58: . . . *good news swapping."* Peters and Waterman, *In Search of Excellence*, p. 124.

Chapter 6

p. 63: . . . *an involuntary conversion of a 727."* Nash and Zullo, *The Mis-Fortune 500*, p. 193.

p. 63: . . . *is a 17-page document."* William Lutz, *Doublespeak: The Use of Language to Deceive You* (New York: HarperPerennial, 1989), p. 163.

p. 63: . . . *as good as an upturn in the downturn."* Ibid., p. 126.

p. 64: . . . *the provincials couldn't understand."* Bill Vlasic and Bradlee Stertz, *Taken for a Ride* (New York: William Morrow, 2000), as quoted in Brock Yates, "Daimler Drives Chrysler into a Ditch," *Wall Street Journal,* 11/8/00.

p. 67: . . . *were rated exemplerary by our own tests." 60 Minutes,* 9/10/00.

p. 67: . . . *phony with a capital F."* Ross Petras and Kathryn Petras, *The 776 Stupidest Things Ever Said* (New York: Main Street Books, 1993), p. 181.

p. 68: . . . *I'm just the one to do it.:* Ibid, p. 36.

p. 68: . . . *like good Christians?"* Ibid, p. 116.

p. 68: . . . *and circle all the mistakes."* Newsweek, 4/00.

p. 71: . . . *guess how this went over.* Petras and Petras, *The 776 Stupidest Things Ever Said*, p. 23.

p. 72: . . . *canceled a planned joint business venture.* Associated Press, 6/6/99.

p. 72: . . . *terminated his lucrative endorsement contract. San Diego Union-Tribune*, 9/17/00.

p. 73: . . . *Kissinger knew better."* Seymour Hersh, *The Price of Power* (New York: Simon & Schuster, 1983), p. 61.

p. 73: . . . *like hiding his head in shame."* James Goldsborough, "Another Sorry Chapter in American Hysteria," *San Diego Union-Tribune*, 9/18/00.

p. 75: . . . *now burn it and write another letter."* Paul Boeller, *Presidential Anecdotes* (New York: Penguin Books, 1982), p. 135.

p. 75: . . . *Not so fast, Lopez."* Jacob Braude, *Braude's Treasury of Wit and Humor* (Englewood Cliffs, NJ: Prentice-Hall, 1964), p. 202.

p. 76: . . . *if he interfered with operations.* "Grudges and Ill Will Pervaded Site of Fatal Stadium Crane Fall," *Engineering News Record*, 11/13/00, p. 11.

p. 78: . . . *an embarrassing lawsuit resulted.* "Wall Street Battle: Seasonal Bias," *USA Today*, 9/15/00, p. 82.

Chapter 7

p. 81: . . . *now in full glaze."* Fitzwater, *Call the Briefing*, p. 262.

p. 81: . . . *and the IOC were sincere.* NBC-TV, 9/15/00.

p. 83: . . . *look 'em square in the eye.' " San Diego Union-Tribune*, 9/25/00.

p. 87: . . . *'It was him.' "* Mary McGrary, "Al Serves Up Bread and Butter," *Washington Post*, 8/20/00, p. B1.

p. 88: . . . *with the United Kingdom even below that. The World Competitiveness Report.* The World Economic Forum and the Institute of Management Development, 1995).

p. 89: . . . *may require several phases and groups.* Sidney M. Jourard,

Disclosing Man to Himself (New York: Van Nostrand Reinhold, 1983).

p. 89: . . . *not through harmony.* John Norton, International Resource Center.

p. 90: . . . *"He licked his knife clean."* Cathy Lubenski, "Show Me the Manners: New Motto Stresses Proper Corporate Conduct," *San Diego Union-Tribune*, 5/2/99, p. D8.

p. 92: . . . *dirty clothing, and filthy hands."* Ken Lloyd, Workplace Q&A column, *San Diego Union-Tribune*, 4/10/00, p. C4.

p. 94: . . . *he's just evicted a widow."* Mike Royko, cited in David Olive, *Political Babble* (New York: John Wiley and Sons, 1992), p. 170.

Chapter 8

p. 102: . . . *Andy Sipowicz wears them all the time."* "Scenes from the Class Struggle in Springfield," *The Simpsons*, aired February 4, 1996, written by Jennifer Crittenden, dir. Susie Dietter, prod. Matt Groening.

p. 103: . . . *they never warmed up to us."* Interview with team member, Honolulu, 1997.

Chapter 10

p. 120: . . . *will soon stop trying to communicate with him."* Lynn Townsend, as quoted in Richard Huseman and associates, *Readings in Interpersonal and Organizational Communication* (Boston: Allyn & Bacon, 1974).

p. 121: . . . *won out over 'overt sucking up.' "* "Poor Prep Work Costs Firms Jobs," *Engineering News Record*, 8/28/00, p. 24.

p. 121: . . . *before he was done."* Life, 7/28/72.

p. 123: . . . *is declared the listener."* Nathan Miller, quoted in Robert Bolton, *People Skills* (Englewood Cliffs, NJ: Prentice-Hall, 1979), p. 4.

p. 124: . . . and becomes a duel-logue." Interview with Paul Sullivan, 6/28/00, Boston.

Chapter 11

p. 139: . . . *bad news was always headed.*" Seymour Hirsch, *The Price of Power* (Summit, 1983), p. 177.

Chapter 13

p. 155: . . . *and get out among his people*" Keith Davis, *Human Behavior at Work: Human Relations and Organizational Behavior* (New York: McGraw-Hill, 1992).

p. 156 . . . *we won't shoot you.* Geoffrey Brewer, "The Best Meeting I Ever Ran," *Performance*, 3/95, p. 51.

p. 160: . . . *he'd eat you alive.*" Nash and Zullo, *The Mis-Fortune 500.*

Chapter 15

p. 185: . . . *'Not good,' he said.*" *Newsweek*, 12/6/99.

Chapter 16

p. 192: . . . *any argument will always be story.*" Gerry Spence, *How to Argue and Win Every Time* (New York: St. Martin's Press, 1995), p. 114.

p. 195: . . . *dogs led to survival and victory.* Brewer, *Performance*, 3/00.

p. 197: *"Well, I'll be damned!"* Joy Dana Wilkie and Toby Sckert, "Lieberman's Warmth Rubs Off on Gore," *San Diego Times-Union*, 9/13/00, p. A9.

p. 200: . . . *Motivate him or her to change behavior.* "It's Not Easy Being an Angel," *Washington Post*, 8/9/00, p. C10.

p. 202: . . . *defending his arms-buildup program.* Olive, *Political Babble*, p. 130.

Chapter 17

p. 213: . . . *smoking in or near tot lots.* Ray Huard, "Kids Butt in, Seek to Clear Air in Parks," *San Diego Union-Tribune*, 10/19/00.

p. 215: . . . *from the shoes of senior managers.* " "In the Office, on the Edge," *San Francisco Chronicle*, 8/22/00, p. A1.

Chapter 18

p. 225: . . . *held up the expanded talks for ten weeks.*" Hersh, *The Price of Power*, p. 55.

p. 228: . . . *Could Woody Allen have written a better script?* "Four Accused of Faking Job Ties in Scheme to Illicitly Acquire $1.6 Million in Gold," *San Diego Union-Tribune*, 12/21/00, p. A4.

p. 233: . . . *One of those days, I guess.* Nash and Zullo, *The Mis-Fortune 500*, p. 59.

p. 235: . . . *but just in case* . . . Maura Reynolds, "Hitler; Fate of Corpse One of War's Mysteries," *Los Angeles Times*, 4/28/00, p. A12.

Chapter 19

p. 248: . . . *a lot of emotion and fire, no question.*" "Fightin' at Foxboro," *San Diego Union-Tribune*, 11/20/00.

Chapter 20

p. 260: . . . *"This is very, very . . . disrespectful.'* " Jeffrey Rabin, "Riders Walk Out of MTA Hearing on Bus Lines," *Los Angeles Times*, 11/19/00.

Chapter 21

p. 267: . . . *but I repeat myself.* Nancy McPhee, *The Book of Insults* (New York: Penguin Books, 1980), p. 116.

p. 267: . . . *Egyptians worshiped an insect.*" Ibid.

p. 268: . . . *a member of his own party.* Olive, *Political Babble*.

p. 268 . . . *since the end of the Middle Ages.*" H. L. Mencken, *Prejudices: A Selection* (Baltimore: Johns Hopkins University Press, 1996).

Index of Famous Lines

Line	*Page*
Alas, poor Yorick	212
All the world's a stage	175
All things are ready, if our minds be so	107
An honest tale speeds best being plainly told	50
Bell, book and candle	31
Beware the Ides of March	153
Brevity is the soul of wit	51
Cowards die many times before their deaths	58
Cry 'Havoc,' and let slip the dogs of war	48
Double, double toil and trouble	226
For the apparel oft proclaims the man	97
For 'tis the mind that makes the body rich	110
Friends, Romans, Countrymen, lend me your ears	180
Give every man thy ear, but few thy voice	120
God give thee the spirit of persuasion	290
Have more than thou showest	183
He draweth out the thread of his verbosity	146
Here's a fellow frights English out of his wits	67
I do desire we be better strangers	249
I do not much dislike the matter, but the manner	79
I summon up remembrance of things past	48
It is a tale told by an idiot	189
It was Greek to me	63
I wasted time, and now doth time waste me	173
Many a good hanging prevents a bad marriage	250
Mend your speech a little	23

Men's faults do seldom to themselves appear   17
Misery acquaints a man with strange bedfellows   246
More matter, with less art   217

Now is the winter of our discontent   58

O, call back yesterday, bid time return   174
Once more unto the breach, dear friends   115, 250
Our remedies oft in ourselves do lie   26
Out, damned spot!   85

Screw your courage to the sticking-place   111
Speak the speech, I pray you   37
Suit the action to the word   85

The evil men do lives after them   236
The fault, dear Brutus, is not in our stars   27
The first thing we do, let's kill all the lawyers   248
The quality of mercy is not strain'd   58
There is nothing either good or bad
    but thinking makes it so   111
There's small choice in rotten apples   247
There is a tide in the affairs of men   26
The sense of death is most in apprehension   107
They have been at a great feast of languages   61
This royal throne of kings, this sceptred isle   47
To fear the worst oft cures the worse   110
To gild refines gold, to paint the lily   217
To thine own self be true   84

We few, we happy few, we band of brothers   241, 291
We have kiss'd away kingdoms and provinces   237
What a piece of work is a man   48
What a spendthrift is he of his tongue!   128
Why, I can smile, and murder whiles I smile   94

You have such a February face   80

Index

Abrasiveness, 258

Acknowledgment, 91

Acronyms, 65

Active tense, 65

Alcohol use, 113–114

Ali, Muhammed, 267

Alienation, appearance and, 104–105

Allen, Woody, 7, 228

All's Well That Ends Well, 9, 26, 86, 100, 267, 290

Antony and Cleopatra, 29, 31, 53, 79, 138–139, 171–172, 237, 242, 275, 278

Anxiety (*see* Nervousness)

Appearance, 97–105
    alienation through, 104–105
    attitude and, 99
    conformity and, 98, 102–104
    first impressions, 97–98, 158
    other factors and, 100–102
    overestimating, 100–101

Apple Macintosh, 230

Argument:
    and critical listening skills, 145–149
    flim-flam detector, 147–149, 183
    importance of sound, 203–204

Aristotle, 49

As You Like It, 5, 17, 49, 87, 100, 103, 123, 135–136, 143, 175–176, 214–215, 224, 226, 249, 266

Attacking, 136

Attitude:
    appearance and, 99
    language and, 55–56
    nervousness and, 107–116
    praise and, 56–58
    upbeat versus downbeat, 55–56

Audience:
    assessment of, 184, 200–201
    connecting with, 167–169
    keeping attention of, 200–202
    noticing response of, 128–130
    understanding target, 161–162, 204
    (*See also* Receivers)

Aznavour, Charles, 42

Backup systems, 234–236

Baker, Tammy Faye, 197

Balfour, Arthur, 68

Bardin, Mary Beth, 195

Barger, Sonny, 200

Barnum, P. T., 146

Belichick, Bill, 248

Benchley, Peter, 199

Benny, Jack, 194

Big words, 65

Blaming, 282–284

Blanchard, Ken, 21, 56–57

Blowing off steam, 277–278

Body language, 79–95
    congruence and, 84–86

Body language (*Cont.*):
  cultural differences in, 87–89
  importance of, 80–81
  in listening process, 125, 129, 131
  liveliness of, 86–87
  lying and, 81, 86, 92–94
  manners and, 90–92
  in Q&A, 137, 142
  reliance on, 81–83
Boeller, Paul, 75
Bogart, Humphrey, 86
Bolton, Robert, 7, 123, 126–127
Brainstorming, 181
Braude, Jacob, 75
Breathing, 112
Brevity, 52, 65–66
Brewer, Geoffrey, 155, 195
Broadcast News (movie), 109
Brooks, Albert, 109
Brooks, Mel, 236
Broughton, Philip, 268
Bush, George, 14–15, 53, 71, 80–81, 194
Bush, George W., 67, 83, 98, 225
Business etiquette, 90–92
Butcher, Susan, 195
Buzz phrases, 268

Cagney, James, 109
Carter, Jimmy, 70, 233
Casey, William, 41–42
Catch 22 (movie), 125
Celebration, 274–275
Cell phones, 232–233

Chairs, comfort of, 225
Challenger accident, 120
Child, Julia, 40
Chrysler, 63–64, 195
Churchill, Winston, 267
Cicero, 204
Clarity, 62–65
Clark, Kathy, 8
Click and Clack, 39
Clinton, Bill, 65, 71, 140, 211, 233
Clothing (*see* Appearance)
Coca-Cola, 172
Comedy of Errors, 156, 266
Communication:
  cultural issues in, 87–89, 125, 204
  evaluation of, 18–20, 25
  feedback on, 18–20, 25
  flow of, 155–157
  importance of, 4–5, 8, 23–26
  nature of good, 13–15
  openness to improving, 17–18, 21, 26–27
  problems in, 6–8, 15–17
  resistance to improving, 27–30
  rewards of improving, 31–32
  role models for, 20–21
  success and, 29–30
Communication model, 32, 33
Communication style, 23–25, 160
  delivery style, 42–43
  of professions, 6
  response style, 124–126
Competitive communication, 239–285
  competitive bids and, 137, 259
  about competitors, 263–270

Competitive communication (*Cont.*):
  losing after, 277–285
  preparation for, 253–261
  teamwork in, 241–251
  winning after, 271–276
Computer graphics software, 212
Computers, 235
Conclusions, 185–186
Conflict resolution, 76
Conformity:
  in appearance, 98, 102–104
  body language and, 87–89
  of message to rules, 176–178
Confrontation, 89, 283
Congruent communication, 84–86
Contracts, 10
Control, 91
Copperfield, David, 213
Coriolanus, 109, 115, 129, 169, 247, 257, 282
Cosell, Howard, 39
Costas, Bob, 38
Courtesy, 91
Credibility, 202
Critical listening, 145–149
Cronkite, Walter, 39
Culture:
  audience response and, 204
  body language and, 87–89
  communication and, 125
Cumming, Candy, 213
Customer service representatives, communication skills of, 6
Cuteness, 140–142
Cymbeline, 70, 107, 145, 284

Daimler-Benz, 63–64
Davis, Keith, 155
Defensiveness, 137, 141–142
Delivery style, 42–43
Demosthenes, 49
Dependability, 91
Dewey, Thomas, 44, 272
Diction, 41–42
Die Hard (movie), 112
Diller, Phyllis, 40
Dirty tricks, 283–284
Disraeli, Benjamin, 267
Dole, Bob, 93–94
Dressing for Success, 99
Drinking, 113–114
Duberstein, Ken, 81
Dukakis, Michael, 65, 140, 194

E-mail, 5
Eastwood, Clint, 39
Eisenhower, Dwight, 73
Emerson, Ralph Waldo, 29
Emotional impact, 49–50
Engineering Education, 8
Engineers, communication skills of, 10, 31–32
Enos, Frank, 156
Environment:
  meeting room, 225–226
  (*See also* Facilities)
Epithets, 266–269
Errors in usage, 67–69
Evaluation, of communication, 18–20, 25

Executive summary, 52, 184, 185
Eye contact, 131–132

Facial expression, 131
Facilitation, domination versus, 126–127
Facilities, 223–237
  assessing comfort of, 224–225
  details concerning, 226–228
  layout of room, 157
  temperature and environment of, 225–226
  visual media and, 228–237
Fair play, 91
Falwell, Jerry, 204
Fault-finding statements, 136
Favoritism, 283–284
Feedback:
  on appearance, 99
  on communication, 18–20, 25
  in communication model, 32
  on competitive presentation, 254–259
  labels and, 73–74
  praise, 56–58
  response style and, 124–126
  from reviewers, 256–259
  to sender from audience, 128–130
  taking seriously, 258–259
  video review in, 20, 255–256
Fellowship, 273–274
Ferraro, Geraldine, 111
Financial professionals, communication skills of, 6

Financial rewards, 167
Finger-pointing, 282–284
First impressions, 97–98, 158
Fitzwater, Marlin, 14–15, 16–17, 53, 80–81
Flim-Flam Man, The (movie), 147
Flow of communication, 155–157
Focus, 51–53
Ford, Gerald, 70–71, 140, 233
Foul language, 77–78, 266–269
Franklin, Ben, 244

Gantt charts, 174
Gates, Bill, 98, 233
Gates, Daryl, 71
General Dynamics, 247
Genuineness, 91
Gloating, 159–160
Gorbachev, Mikhail, 147
Gore, Al, 83, 87, 98, 127, 225
Greenspan, Alan, 70–71
Grooming, 91, 114–115
GTE, 195

Hamlet, 5, 10, 19, 20, 25, 28, 37, 43, 48, 51–52, 64, 76, 82, 84, 85, 92, 97, 102, 108, 111, 120, 140–141, 142–143, 167, 176, 184, 190, 199, 212–213, 217, 234, 235–237, 253, 255, 258, 271, 272, 276, 277
Hands-on experience, 214–216
Harding, Tonya, 77

Hardship stories, 197

Harvey, Paul, 38

Henry IV, Part 1, 6–7, 53–54, 84–85, 90, 104, 109, 128, 159, 202, 224, 243–244, 249, 257, 265, 267, 272, 275, 281, 282, 283, 290

Henry IV, Part 2, 10, 13, 44, 77, 100, 113, 119, 148, 155, 248, 249, 267, 271, 276

Henry V, 14, 15, 24, 107, 115, 123, 153, 185, 194, 195, 219, 230, 241, 250, 284, 291–292

Henry VI, Part 1, 9, 49, 129, 140, 274

Henry VI, Part 2, 15, 76, 81, 104, 173, 215–216, 220, 256, 278, 281

Henry VI, Part 3, 24, 94, 186, 189, 215, 220–221, 275

Henry VIII, 18, 92, 197, 280, 284

Hersh, Seymour, 73, 139, 225

Hill, Anita, 204

Hitchcock, Alfred, 199

Hitler, Adolf, 235

Holbrook, Hal, 200–201

Honesty, 91

Hot buttons, 198–199

Huard, Ray, 213

Humor, 89, 196–197, 204

Hygiene, 91, 114–115

Images, through language, 53–55, 193–194

Information channels, 155–157

Information overload, 183–184

International Olympic Committee, 81

International Resource Center, 89

Interrupting, 123–124

Investment professionals, communication skills of, 6

Jacobi, Jeffrey, 40–41

Jaws (movie), 199

Jesus, 229

Johnson, Lyndon B., 77, 247

Johnson, Magic, 93

Jones, James Earl, 38

Jourard, Sidney, 88–89

Juarez, Cirilo, 260

Judges, communication skills of, 10

Julius Caesar, 26, 27, 48, 58, 63, 93, 153, 154, 159, 170, 179, 180, 190–191, 198–199, 216, 236, 245, 258, 275

Jury members, communication skills of, 10–11

"Just-in-case" materials, 184

Kearns, David, 156

Keillor, Garrison, 192

Kemp, Shawn, 72

Kennedy, John F., 140, 247

Kennedy, Ted, 140

King John, 11, 15, 18, 31, 48, 65, 111, 130, 148, 217, 233

King Lear, 10, 23, 38, 42, 155, 166, 183, 242, 264, 280–281

Kissinger, Henry, 40, 73, 139

Knight, Bobby, 77
Knotts, Don, 40

Labels, 73–74
Laird, Melvin, 73
Language, 47–78
    attitude and, 55–56
    blunt-instrument approach and, 74–75
    brevity of, 52, 65–66
    clarity of, 62–65
    emotional impact of, 49–50
    failure to speak up, 72–73
    focus and, 51–53
    foul, 77–78, 266–269
    heavy-handedness in, 75–77
    improving, 68–69
    labeling and, 73–74
    lasting power of, 48
    painting pictures with, 53–55, 193–194
    plain, 50–51
    power of, 58–59
    praise and, 56–58
    thinking before speaking, 70–72
    usage errors and, 67–69
    visual images in, 53–55, 193–194
    wordiness and, 61–62
    (See also Body language)
Laser printers, 235
Law enforcement professionals, communication skills of, 6
Lawyers, communication skills of, 6, 10

Layout of room, 157
Leaders:
    communication skills of, 10
    team, 245–246, 247–249
    winning and, 273–274
Leapfrog meetings, 157
Lee, Peggy, 280
Leech, Tom, 204
Letting go, after losing, 279–280
Levin, Carl, 71
Licking wounds, after losing, 278–279
Lieberman, Joe, 196–197
Likert, Rensis, 57
Lincoln, Abraham, 74–75, 229
Listening skills, 119–149
    absorption with self and, 128
    body language and, 125, 129, 131
    critical, 145–149
    diagnosing, 120–124
    facilitation versus domination, 126–127
    gloating versus, 159–160
    importance of, 121
    improving, 130–132
    letting others talk, 123–124
    noting audience response, 128–130
    in Q&A, 135–144
    response style and, 124–126
    sense of hearing and, 119–120
Lloyd, Ken, 92
Lockheed Corporation, 233
Logic of message, 182–183
Loren, Sophia, 42
Los Angeles MTA (Metropolitan Transit Authority), 260

Losing in competitive communication, 277–285
  blame and, 282–284
  blowing off steam, 277–278
  letting go, 279–280
  licking wounds, 278–279
  paying the piper, 281–282
  self-abuse and, 280–281
Love's Labour's Lost, 4, 19, 44, 61, 66, 119, 124, 141, 146, 182, 203, 204, 233, 282
Lutz, William, 63
Lying, body language and, 81, 86, 92–94

McAuliffe, Anthony, 50
Macbeth, 72, 85, 94, 103, 111, 139, 157–158, 165, 167, 178, 180–181, 189, 223, 226–227, 246, 274, 276, 279, 289
McCain, John, 140
McCarthy, Joe, 73
McDonnell Douglas, 247
McGovern, George, 121
McGrory, Mary, 87
McLuhan, Marshall, 218, 231
McPhee, Nancy, 267
Macrone, Michael, 50
Maguire, Jerry, 268–269
Mailer, Norman, 121
Main points, 190–191
Major, John, 185
Malone, Sam, 155–156
Mannerisms, 45

Manners, 90–92
Marshall, George, 73
Maslow, Abraham, 167
MBWA (Management by Wandering Around), 153–154
Measure for Measure, 10–11, 15, 27, 69, 107, 114, 211
Medical professionals, communication skills of, 6
Medium, 207–237
  in communication model, 32, 33
  facility and, 223–237
  Murphy's Law and, 227, 233–234, 236
  visual aids as, 66, 209–221
Meetings:
  environment for, 225–226
  leapfrog, 157
  problems of, 8
  techniques for running, 21
  (*See also* Facilities)
Mehrabian, Albert, 82
Mencken, H. L., 268
Merchant of Venice, The, 10, 19, 30, 39, 58, 61, 83, 102, 147, 174, 186, 202, 273, 281
Merry Wives of Windsor, The, 67, 68, 135, 259, 260, 273–274, 283, 289
Message, 151–205
  audience focus on, 200–201
  in communication model, 32, 33
  conclusions to, 185–186
  credibility of, 202
  cultural differences and, 204
  fitting to rules, 176–178

Message (*Cont.*):
  gloating and, 159–160
  hot buttons in, 198–199
  humor in, 196–197, 204
  ignoring market warnings and, 171–173
  information channels and, 155–157
  information overload and, 183–184
  information snags and, 154–155
  knowing territory of, 153–154
  logic of, 182–183
  main points of, 190–191
  objective of, 165–167
  opener for, 178–180
  planning and, 170–171, 173–174
  respect and, 91, 169
  rushing to judgment and, 160–161
  scorn and, 157–159
  sorting information for, 175–176
  sound argument versus sound in, 203–204
  storytelling and, 191–193, 197–202
  structure of, 180–182
  summarizing, 52, 184, 185
  understanding target audience and, 161–162
  visual imagery in, 53–55, 193–194
  vivid support in, 195
  wavelength of listeners and, 167–169
Metaphors, 65
Midsummer Night's Dream, A, 15, 38, 39, 101, 114, 224, 253, 254
Mikulski, Barbara, 39
Miller, Nathan, 123
Milloy, Lawyer, 248

Mindmapping, 181
Mironenko, Sergei, 235
Mixed messages, 85
Monty Python, 124
Motion, in visual aids, 212
Motivation, 167
Motley Fool, 200
Much Ado About Nothing, 29, 40, 50, 80, 83, 108, 126, 129, 175, 178, 186, 266, 272, 277, 278, 292
Murphy's Law, 227, 233–234, 236
Murray, Bill, 248
Music Man, The (movie), 154
Mutiny on the Bounty (movie), 86

Name-calling, 73–74
Nash, Bruce, 55, 63, 160
Nervousness, 107–116
  drinking and, 113–114
  grooming and, 114–115
  nature of, 107–109
  positive aspect of, 109–110
  positive attitude and, 115
  preventing, 110–112
  sleep problems and, 113
New England Patriots, 248
Newhart, Bob, 125
Nicholson, Jack, 39
Nike, 172–173
Nixon, Richard, 73, 77, 139, 225, 247
Nonverbal communication (*see* Body language)
Northrop Grumman, 21

Norton, John, 89
Note-taking, 132

Objective, of message, 165–167
Olive, David, 94, 202, 268
O'Neal, Shaquille, 255
Open-door policies, 125, 155
Openers, 178–180
Othello, 30, 43, 70, 71, 74, 108, 114, 147, 160, 193, 227, 231, 244, 245, 256, 263, 274, 277, 280
Outlining, 181

Pachter, Barbara, 90
Palm Pilot, 230
Parker, John, 68
Passive tense, 65
Paying the piper, after losing, 281–282
Pepper, Claude, 265–266
Perez, Rosie, 39
Perfectionism, 248
Pericles, 97, 214
Perot, Ross, 40, 210
Peters, Tom, 18, 57–58, 192
Petras, Ross and Kathryn, 71
Pfeiffers Brewing Co., 55
Philip of Macedon, 50
Philosophers, communication skills of, 11
Physicians, communication skills of, 11
Picturesque language, 53–55, 193–194
Plain talk, 50–51
Planning, of message, 170–171, 173–174

Politicians, communication skills of, 6, 10
Politics, 283–284
Praise, 56–58
Preachers, communication skills of, 10
Preparation:
    of competitive presentation, 259–260
    planning of message, 170–171, 173–174
Price Club, 173
Problem-solving meetings, 137
Procrastination, 110, 173, 253
Professionalism, punctuality and, 259–260
Professions, communication styles of, 6
Project management, 174
Projection, of voice, 39–40
Projectors, 233, 235, 259
Props, 212–214, 218–219, 220–221
Pseudo questions, 137
Psycho (movie), 199
Public address system, 233
Punctuality, 259–260
Putdowns, 77–78

Q&A (question and answer), 135–144
    body language in, 137, 142
    cuteness in, 140–142
    questioner role in, 135–139
    responder role in, 139–140
    successful, 142–144
    tips for surviving, 144
Qualcomm, 173
Quayle, Dan, 67

Questioner:
  nature of questions, 136–137
  in Q&A, 135–139
  stifling of questions by, 135–139
Quinn, Anthony, 42

Rape of Lucrece, The, 17, 209
Rashomon (movie), 160
Rathbone, Basil, 47–48
Reading aloud, 44, 45
Reagan, Ronald, 77, 140, 147, 202
Real estate professionals, communication skills of, 6
Receivers:
  body language of sender and, 80
  in communication model, 32, 33
  connecting with, 167–169
  information snags and, 154–155
  as questioners in Q&A, 135–139
  as responders in Q&A, 139–140
  (*See also* Audience; Listening skills)
Reebok, 72
Reflective listening, 127
Rehearsal, 253–259
  feedback and, 254–259
  importance of, 253–254
Reiner, Rob, 197
Requests for proposals (RFPs), 259
Respect, 91, 169
Responder, in Q&A, 139–140
Response style, 124–126
Revenge, 258
Reviewers, 256–259
Reynolds, Maura, 235

Richard II, 14, 47, 55, 84, 173, 174, 191, 264
Richard III, 24, 41, 50, 52, 58–59, 80, 113, 145, 266, 282, 284
Richards, Ann, 194
Rivera, Geraldo, 203
Rivers, Joan, 267
Robert Half International, 8
Robertson, Pat, 71–72
Rockefeller, Nelson, 247
Rocker, John, 77
Rogers, Carl, 122
Rogers, William, 73
Role plays, 122–123
Romeo and Juliet, 183, 203, 225, 265
Roosevelt, Eleanor, 43–44
Roosevelt, Theodore, 268
Rosanne, 40
Royko, Mike, 93–94
Russell, Bill, 245–246

Salesmen, communication skills of, 6
Scary stories, 199–200
Scheduling, 174
Schlesinger, Laura, 77–78
Schwarzkopf, Norman, 210
Scorn, 157–159
Scott, George C., 147
Scoundrels:
  communication and, 15–17
  competition and, 263–264
Scully, Vincent, 39
Self-talk, positive, 111

Sender, 35–116
  appearance of, 97–105
  awareness of audience response, 128–130
  body language of, 79–95
  in communication model, 32, 33
  information snags and, 154
  language of, 47–78
  positive attitude of, 107–116
  as questioner in Q&A, 135–139
  as responder in Q&A, 139–140
  voice of, 37–45
Serling, Rod, 39, 199
Shelton, Henry, 71
Sihanouk, Prince, 139
Simmons, Richard, 40
Simon, Carly, 109
Simpson, O. J., 218
Simpsons, 40, 102
Singing, 44
Sleep:
  catching up on, 275–276
  problems with, 113
Smathers, George, 265
Smiling, 93–94
Smoking, 44, 199–200, 213, 226
Social manners, 91
Society for Marketing Professional
    Services, 121
Sonnet 23, 110
Sonnet 29, 279
Sonnet 30, 48
Sonnet 76, 229
Speaking up:
  about competition, 263–270

Speaking up (*Cont.*):
  failure to speak up, 72–73
  information channels and, 155–157
  whistle blowing, 120
Speaks, Larry, 14
Spence, Gerry, 192
Sprewell, Latrell, 76
Stern-Leach Company, 228
Stertz, Bradlee, 63–64
Storyboarding, 181
Storytelling, 191–193, 197–202
Stossel, John, 109
Streisand, Barbra, 109
Stripes (movie), 248
Structure of message, 180–182
Struthers, Sally, 197
Sullivan, Paul, 124
Summarizing message, 52, 184, 185
Sununu, John, 16–17
Supporting information, 191–200
Supreme Court, 64
Swift, Jonathan, 204

Take the Money and Run (movie), 7
Taming of the Shrew, The, 75, 110,
    128, 209, 228, 247, 264
Teachers, communication skills of, 6
Teamwork, 241–251
  camaraderie and, 242, 273–274
  leaders and, 245–246, 247–249
  losing in competitive communication
    and, 277–285
  problems with, 243–244, 249–250
  success with, 244–246

Teamwork (*Cont.*):
  team composition and, 246–247
  winning in competitive competition
    and, 271–276
Techies, communication skills of, 6, 8,
    10, 31–32
Telemarketing representatives, commu-
    nication skills of, 6
Telephones:
  automated phone systems, 232
  cell phones, 232–233
Temperature, meeting room, 225–226
Tempest, The, 15, 76, 128, 130, 243,
    244, 246, 258, 273, 282
Terms, 65
Thanking others, 272–273
Thomas, Clarence, 204
360 degree feedback, 18
Timon of Athens, 11, 17, 267, 279
Toastmasters Club, 45
Townsend, Lynn, 120
Training sessions, 137
Travel itinerary, 235
Troilus and Cressida, 3, 61, 79, 110,
    136, 165, 168, 212, 263, 267,
    284
Truman, Harry, 44, 267, 272
Turner, Kathleen, 39
Tutu, Desmond, 42
Twain, Mark, 200–201, 267
Twelfth Night, 15, 25, 56, 196, 250,
    283, 290
Two Gentlemen of Verona, The, 28,
    90
Two Noble Kinsmen, 185, 218
Tyson, Mike, 77

USA Today, 210
Usage errors, 67–69

Ventura, Jesse, 213
Venus and Adonis, 4, 177
Victory party, 274–275
Video review, 20, 255–256
Visual aids, 66, 209–221
  backfiring of, 217–218
  basic keys to using, 211
  hands-on experience and, 214–216
  importance of, 209–211
  motion and, 212
  overdoing, 217–218
  props as, 212–214, 218–219, 220–
    221
  visual media options, 228–237
Visual imagery, 53–55, 193–194
Visualization, 112, 179
Vlasic, Bill, 63–64
Voice, 37–45
  appeal of, 38–39
  diction and, 41–42
  information revealed in, 42–43
  mannerisms and, 45
  other factors and, 43–44
  perking up, 44–45
  projection of, 39–40
  quality of, 40–41

Wallace, George, 267
Walton, Bill, 31
Warner, John, 71

Warnings, ignoring market, 171–173
Waterman, Robert, 18, 57–58
Watt, James, 77
Weekend at Bernie's (movie), 216
Weitz, John, 115
Wendel, Sharon, 31–32
Whistle blowers, 120, 263–270
Williams, Venus, 254
Willis, Bruce, 112
Winfrey, Oprah, 38
Winning in competitive communication, 271–276
  celebration and, 274–275
  fellowship in, 273–274

Winning in competitive communication (*Cont.*):
  sleep and, 275–276
  thanks in, 272–273
Winters, Jonathan, 40
Winter's Tale, The, 62, 73, 79–80, 99, 101, 192, 269, 278
Woods, Tiger, 83, 254
Woodward, Bob, 41–42
Wordiness, 61–62
Wright, Frank Lloyd, 42

Yeltsin, Boris, 185

Zullo, Allan, 55, 63, 160

About the Author

Thomas Leech is one of today's most sought-after consultants on business communications, public speaking, and presentations. His clients for executive and team coaching, training seminars, and conference programs include many Fortune 500 companies, public agencies, and professional associations. He conducts the team presentation module for the University of California–San Diego (UCSD) Extension Executive Leadership Programs and has taught management communications for National University. He served as communications administrator for General Dynamics and was one of the nation's first corporate ombudsmen. He is a long-time freelance writer and columnist, with over 200 articles on communication in *Presentations*, *Master Salesman*, *Manage*, *The Toastmaster*, and business journals, plus the monthly Outdoors Forum for *San Diego* magazine's online edition, San Diego Online. He's the author of *How to Prepare, Stage & Deliver Winning Presentations*, which won a "Best Business Book of the Year" award from Library Journal. He welcomes your comments and inquiries; send via e-mail to bardTL@aol.com.